TOO LITTLE TOO LATE?

TOO LITTLE TOO LATE?

The Challenges That Still Face British Education

JOHN RAE

COLLINS
8 Grafton Street, London W1
1989

William Collins Sons & Co. Ltd
London · Glasgow · Sydney · Auckland
Toronto · Johannesburg

BRITISH LIBRARY CATALOGUING IN PUBLICATION DATA

Rae, John, *1931–*
Too little too late?: the challenges that still face
British education.
1. Great Britain. Education. Policies of government
I. Title
379.41

ISBN 0 00 215082 4

First published in Great Britain by
William Collins 1989
Copyright © John Rae 1989

Typeset in Janson by
Ace Filmsetting Ltd, Frome, Somerset
Made and printed in Great Britain by
William Collins Sons & Co. Ltd, Glasgow

TO
MY GRANDDAUGHTER
FRANCESCA

'We call those studies "liberal" which are worthy of a free man; those studies by which we attain and practise virtue and wisdom; that education which calls forth, trains and develops those highest gifts of body and mind which ennoble man . . .'

VITTORINO DA FELTRE, 15th-century humanist

'Let us have a common education for all alike. Everything grows narrow under a domestic education; everything expands under public education. I too am a father; but my son does not belong to me. He belongs to the Republic. It is for her to decide what he ought to do in order to serve her well.'

GEORGES DANTON, to the French Revolutionary
Convention, 1793

'It is no use trying to give technical teaching to our artisans without elementary education; uneducated labourers – and many of our labourers are utterly uneducated – are for the most part unskilled labourers, and if we have our work-folk any longer unskilled, notwithstanding their strong sinews and determined energy, they will become over-matched in the competition of the world.'

W. E. FORSTER, President of the Board of
Education, to the British House of Commons, 1870

'Education is not for the sake of the student but for the sake of the state.'

MORI ARINORI, Japanese Minister of
Education, 1885–9

'The Soviet school is required to produce well-rounded people who know their school subjects well but who are at the same time capable of useful labour; it must develop in young people an urge to be useful to society and participate actively in the production of the wealth which society needs.'

NIKITA KHRUSHCHEV, to the 13th Congress of
the Soviet Komsomol, 1958

'The National Curriculum will mean that boys and girls cannot opt out of technology until they are 16, which means that even those who are academically gifted will have to roll up their sleeves and learn some craft. We have for far too long in our country under-estimated the importance of craft skills.'

KENNETH BAKER, Secretary of State for
Education and Science, in an interview with
The Times, 2 September 1988

CONTENTS

FOREWORD

This book is an argument, a tract if you like, about the condition of British education. It is not intended to be a scholarly work or an objective analysis, but to propose the motion that our education system is still in need of major reform. My starting point is the Education Reform Act of 1988, the most important and far-reaching education act since the state took responsibility for public education in 1870; and I ask how far the Act meets and fails to meet the economic and social needs of our society.

But the book is not a study of the Education Reform Act. It does not deal with those sections of the Act that affect the universities. I am interested in schools: how good schools are created, what they need to teach, how they should teach, and how the school system should be organized. It is central to my argument that these questions should be considered in their international as well as in their domestic context. It is also central to my argument that we will not come up with the right answers unless we are clear what we want the outcome of education to be.

Anyone who sets out to express a view on what the aims of British education should be and how those aims can be achieved is likely to provoke the question, 'Who does he think he is?' This is especially true if the writer is the former headmaster of an independent school. The independent schools are not only outside the national system of education; they have for the most part remained silent on the controversies that have divided British education since the War. By doing so, they have encouraged the view, already held by many who work in the state sector, that the heads of independent schools are the last people who should comment on the schools that educate the majority of children.

I did not accept the view when I was working in the independent sector, and I do not accept it now. I am too interested in education to remain silent, particularly at this critical point in the history of our school system. I do not pretend to be an expert on every aspect of education, but I know enough to say where I *think* we have gone wrong, and what steps are needed to put us on the right path. My purpose in writing this book is to test my argument in the forum of public debate.

I am not writing primarily for those directly involved in education. I am writing for all who are concerned about the connection between education and the future of our society. There was a time when people in Britain did not think that connection mattered much; schooling was a rite of passage for the individual, not a means to an end for the country. But that time has passed. Most people today, including teachers, recognize that unless we get our education system right, our future prosperity and social cohesion cannot be guaranteed.

It is to these people that I address my argument. As far as possible I have avoided the sort of jargon that educationalists use to disguise the fact that their subject is largely a matter of common sense. There are some points of nomenclature that I should clarify. I have used the term 'independent schools' rather than the old-style 'public schools' unless I am referring to a period when only the latter rings true; and I have used the term 'state schools' rather than 'maintained schools' because the schools to which the majority of children go *are* part of the state's education provision even though they may be maintained by the local education authority. I have also spoken of 'British education', because the issues I discuss concern the whole United Kingdom, even though education in Scotland and Northern Ireland is different in some respects from that in England and Wales, and is not the direct responsibility of the Secretary of State for Education and Science.

JOHN RAE
August 1988

1

HOW DID WE GET TO WHERE WE ARE?

'That sort of thing is all over now'?

It was July 1945. The war with Germany was over and a Labour government had come to power in Britain with a mandate to put an end to privilege. I took a taxi to the station with my suitcase and tuckbox on the seat beside me. As the school rules required, I was dressed in a school blazer and grey flannels and was carrying my straw hat. I was fourteen and this was the end of my first year as a boarder at my public school.

At the station, I put on my straw hat and carried my luggage to the ticket office. I looked round for a porter. When I spotted one, I went up to him and asked him to put my luggage on the London train. 'You'll have to take it yourself,' he replied. 'That sort of thing is all over now.'

I must have been aware that Labour's election landslide posed a threat to the sort of school my blazer and straw hat represented. But I doubt whether I had expected the revolution to start so soon. The porter clearly believed that a new age had dawned when public schools would be done away with or made irrelevant by the provision of state schools that were just as good or better. What was 'over' as far as he was concerned was not just fetching and carrying for young public school boys but a whole world of privilege and unequal opportunity.

It was a false dawn. Forty years on, the public schools – or independent schools as they now prefer to be called – are flourishing as never before, while the state schools on which so many people in 1945 pinned their hopes for a better society, are widely judged to have failed the very children they were intended to help.

Those who work in state schools will challenge that statement. They will claim that the education offered in today's state schools is better than in 1945. But they miss the point. Whether today's state-school education is or is not better than forty years ago is irrelevant to today's pupils and today's society. What matters is the *relative* quality of today's education. Is it good enough to ensure that the products of state schools can compete successfully with the products of independent schools for well-paid jobs and for places at the most prestigious universities? Is it good enough to ensure that Britain can compete successfully with the well-educated populations of West Germany and Japan? Even the most loyal supporter of state education would find it difficult to answer those questions with a resounding affirmative. Quality education for all seems as far away as ever.

It is not my purpose to write a history of the last forty years but I cannot ignore the period altogether. The problems that beset British education today have either been created by or compounded by those four decades of false hopes and increasing despair.

War has a number of beneficial side-effects, one of which is to stimulate educational reform. Far-reaching education acts appear to fulfil so many of the needs of a nation fighting for its survival: the need to believe in the possibility of a better society after war, the need to justify the loss of life by giving wider opportunities to the children, and the need to win the peace. The 1944 Education Act was no exception. Out of the war against Nazism would come, not a 'home fit for heroes' as in 1918, but a society in which the children of heroes would be given the best possible start in life. At the time, and long after, the 1944 Act was regarded as a milestone in the history of British education and as one of the important social reforms of the war-time national Government. The minister responsible, R. A. Butler, believed that the Act was his finest political achievement. When he retired from politics and became Master of Trinity College, Cambridge, he also became a governor of Westminster School. He could seldom resist talking about his role in the making of the 1944 Act, indeed there were times when this seemed to be his only topic of conversation. He seemed unaware that this monument had already begun to crumble as its flaws were exposed.

What the Butler Act did achieve was the creation of the first national system of free education in Britain. The system was based on local authorities who were given the responsibility of maintaining primary and secondary schools in their district. The Act did not specify the different types of secondary school, or say how children were to be selected for one type or another. By these omissions, the Act endorsed by implication the recommendations of pre-war reports on education. These were that selection should be based on an intelligence test at the age of eleven and that there should be three types of secondary school: grammar schools for the academically inclined, secondary modern schools for the less academically inclined, and the technical schools for those whose aptitude lay in that direction. The Butler Act thus gave British education its two most significant characteristics: first, that education was primarily a local responsibility in which the central government should have little or no say; and secondly, that children could be divided by innate ability into distinct groups that should receive a particular type and quality of education. In the traditional attitudes that lay behind these characteristics – dislike of strong central government, and belief in a ruling elite who required a different education from the masses – we may find the origins of so much that was and still is wrong with our education system. When the Act was on the statute book, Winston Churchill sent Butler a telegram of congratulations, telling him that he had 'achieved a permanent place in the history of British education'. It is easy to mock complacency from the vantage point of the future but in the case of the 1944 Education Act the mutual congratulations do seem to have been more than usually short-sighted. The catalogue of the Act's failings makes melancholy reading.

The gesture towards technical education was perfunctory and did not work anyway. Few of the technical secondary schools ever got off the ground. It has taken forty years for the British to wake up to the need for technical education for all children, and in that time industrial competitors who had already grasped the importance of technical education have raced ahead.

The failure to take technical education seriously reflected the attitudes of the British Establishment, most of whom had been educated in the humanities at the ancient universities of Oxford and Cambridge. They had been brought up to regard technical education as inferior. At their public schools, the only practical subject other than art was carpentry, whose brown-coated instructors were not allowed to enter the masters' common room.

The same high-minded members of the Establishment endorsed the fact that the Butler Act had nothing to say about what should be taught in schools, except – a supreme irrelevance in the circumstances – to make religion the one compulsory subject. The civil servants and politicians were educational purists. Education was an end in itself: if it could be said to have a goal, this could only be expressed in terms of general enlightenment. Hence the Act required local education authorities 'to contribute towards the spiritual, moral, mental and physical development of the community'. It would be difficult to think of a statement of educational aims that bore less relation to the needs of a country that had been weakened by war and that now had to pay its way in the world. But it was as far as the British were prepared to go towards the central direction of the curriculum. Once again, it has taken forty years for a British government to decide that it ought to be specific in prescribing the content of education.

In their opposition to any central direction of the curriculum, the Establishment had allies in the Labour members of the war-time coalition whose political experience had been almost exclusively in local government. In 1945, the idea of a national curriculum was anathema to all political parties and to all interest groups in education. A national curriculum was associated with foreign education systems, notably that of the French. It also had obvious echoes of education in Nazi Germany. Above all, it was alien to the British tradition that liberty could not be reconciled with a strong central authority.

When the Act spoke of the Minister's duty 'to secure the effective execution by local authorities, under his control and direction, of the national policy . . .' it did not mean direction of the curriculum. Indeed it is difficult to see what these strong words did mean. The key to the system set up by the Butler Act was unquestioning faith in the good sense and competence of local authorities. It does not seem to have occurred to anyone that some local authorities might pursue policies that were totally at odds with the wishes of the central government. When this happened in the 1980s, the public woke up to the fact that without new legislation there was nothing that the Secretary of State for Education could do about it.

A similar naivety lay behind the belief that parents would accept the spirit of the Act, that is, that the grammar and secondary modern school, though different, would be equal in status. There never was the remotest chance that the different types of school would enjoy what officials piously called 'parity of esteem'. From the start, parents had no doubt that the grammar schools were superior and they wanted their children to go to them. The selection process at 11+ was popularly understood to be dividing the sheep from the goats, the future university candidates from the boys and girls who would leave schools at 15 and go into a job.

Why were the enthusiasts for the Act so blind? Harold Dent, a professor of education and one of the Act's most ardent supporters, wrote long after: 'I cannot imagine why we did not foresee what would happen.' And he added the revealing comment: 'We forgot that it has always been impossible to restrain the ambitions of socially ambitious parents for their young and to defeat their manoeuvres.' In other words, the whole basis on which post-war education was built failed to take into account the most natural and predictable desire of parents to get the best for their children. This combination of arrogance and naivety on the part of education theorists and planners is something that has become all too familiar in our own time. It also helps to explain how we have got to where we are.

The attack on selection at 11+

The limitations of the 1944 Act made it inevitable that in the decades that followed education would become a battleground. As the majority of children failed to be selected for a grammar school at 11+, opposition to dividing children into different streams at this early age gathered momentum. The idea of the comprehensive school that would provide for or comprehend the needs of children of all abilities was born.

It was not until the 1960s, however, that the comprehensive 'Movement' was powerful enough to start the educational revolution in its favour. By that time the controversy over selection at 11+ was being fuelled by the conflict between traditional and progressive education.

The best way of understanding the developing struggle in education is to divide the years between 1944 and the present day into three phases. The first phase is the popular movement against selection at 11+ and for comprehensive schools in the Fifties and Sixties. The second phase, which coincided roughly with the Sixties, is the increasing acceptance of progressive education. The third phase is the counter-revolution against both the comprehensive schools and progressive education which started with the publication of the first Black Paper in 1969 and is still continuing twenty years later.

Outside the struggle but a target for those politically committed to ending privilege or ideologically committed to ending elitism and traditional education, were the independent schools. On the whole, the 11+ selection worked in the independent schools' favour. Middle class families that might have been tempted to use the state schools opted for the independent sector rather than face the possible humiliation of their child being sent to a secondary modern school. In the post-war period some of the more obscure independent schools were kept in business by the refugees from the 11+.

As the state sector began to go comprehensive, it was at first thought that the flow of refugees would diminish. For a few years in the Sixties it looked as though this would indeed happen. In some areas, it became almost fashionable to have a child at the local comprehensive. But middle-class enthusiasm for comprehensive schools soon passed. The threat to independent schools, such as it was, disappeared.

Those who were fighting to abolish the 11+ did not concern themselves with the effect of their campaign on the independent schools. No doubt many of them hoped that the independent schools themselves would be abolished before long. Meanwhile, the priority was to remove selection from the state sector. Their most powerful motivation was social and political, not educational. They did not know, no one knew, whether the comprehensive schools would provide a better education, always supposing that this could be defined. But they believed that the end of selection would help to create a more unified society. The division of children at 11+ was seen as a *class* division: abolish the 11+ selection and Britain would have taken an important step towards a classless society.

It was not just the Socialists who thought and argued in these terms. The ideal of a classless society appealed to many people who had no political commitment but who disliked the snobbery they associated with pre-war Britain and hoped that the abolition of class would help to release the energies of the British people.

Another motive behind the attack on the 11+ and the grammar schools was the fashionable dislike of the idea of an elite, a select cadre of citizens who are better fitted by their education and background to rule the country. The ruling elite in Britain was for the most part from the independent schools rather than the grammar schools but it was the grammar schools that provoked the greater hostility. Parents whose children were consigned to the secondary modern schools did not resent the independent schools, which were remote, so much as the grammar schools which gave local people ideas above their station.

The dream of a classless society and the dislike of elites were characteristic of a view of society that in the Sixties was increasingly referred to as egalitarian. Some egalitarians were political activists working through the school system to achieve the downfall of the bourgeois society. The abolition of the 11+ and the grammar schools would be one way of undermining the power and influence of the bourgeoisie. But most egalitarians were utopian not political. They worked for abstract goals such as 'fairness' and 'social justice'. It seemed to them unfair that some children should be more intelligent than others, particularly as intelligence, unlike wealth or power, could not be redistributed. The unfairness could be mitigated, however, if all children went to the same schools and sat in the same class. The comprehensive school was seen as both an instrument for achieving fairness and a theatre in which fairness could be acted out with beneficial results for all concerned – greater confidence for the less intelligent, greater humility for the more intelligent.

A more down-to-earth objection to the 11+ was that it was not foolproof. Affluent parents could increase their children's chance of success by paying for private coaching. Some primary school heads believed in practice tests while others did not. Some intelligent children panicked on the day; some less intelligent children kept their heads and passed. It was even claimed that when the children of local councillors failed, they turned up in the grammar school nevertheless.

The advocates of change were able to juxtapose a glowing prospectus of the comprehensive schools. Parents were promised that the sheer size of the comprehensive school would be an advantage, enabling the schools to offer a much wider range of subjects. No one appears to have thought that it might be sensible to test this sort of promise by introducing a few comprehensives for an experimental period. If this had been done, many of the promises, including the wider choice of subjects, would have been seen to be misleading.

By the mid-Sixties, the tide of public opinion had turned decisively in favour of the comprehensive schools. Some local authorities had already 'gone comprehensive'. Others were planning to do so. The return of a Labour government in 1964 committed to comprehensive schools, accelerated the process: Labour's Education Secretary, Tony Crosland, issued a circular requiring all areas to submit plans for introducing comprehensive schools and phasing out selection.

The strength of Labour's hostility to selection was expressed by the Prime Minister, Harold Wilson, in his speech to the 1967 party conference. Wilson told delegates of his government's 'determination to end the vicious system under which the educational future of a child can be determined by an arbitrary and unscientific test at the incredible age of eleven'. I do not think Wilson believed a word of what he was saying. He was a grammar-school boy himself, and had once said that such schools would disappear over his dead body. When I was headmaster of Westminster, I got to know him well. In all our conversations, the only interest he ever showed in education was to express his admiration for highly selective schools, such as Westminster.

Wilson's lack of interest in education allowed him to be swept along on the popular zeal to see the comprehensive revolution through to its conclusion. One of the last acts of his government in 1970 was to introduce a law to force – in Wilson's words – 'laggard local authorities to come into line with government policy'. It looked as though the struggle against selection at eleven and the grammar schools had been won.

Progressive education on the march

Meanwhile, the other struggle, between traditional and progressive education, had been joined. It is convenient to treat the two struggles separately, but in practice the bitter hostility of progressive education to the whole ethos of the grammar schools was part of the attack on the selection process that provided the grammar schools with their pupils.

Progressive education is a portmanteau expression for a variety of reforms in teaching method, in discipline, in the curriculum and in the internal organization of schools, that have as their common denominator a greater concern for – critics would say 'indulgence of' – the wishes of the child. 'Child-centred education' was the rallying cry. Progressive education was thus a revolt against what was seen as the authoritarian style of traditional education. Every aspect of the traditional approach came under attack, from streaming by ability to the teaching of English grammar, from school uniform to school prizes.

The motivation for this revolt against traditional methods of education was similar to the motivation that led to the attack on the grammar schools and the 11+. Traditional education, with its emphasis on formality, was regarded as elitist. The revolt was also part of the wider rebellion against authority that occurred in the Sixties: traditional education and the didactic teacher who purveyed it were obvious targets, like parents and the police, in an age when no authority could be taken for granted.

Progressive education was thus a response to the mood of the times. But the source of those progressive ideas that are still so fiercely debated, lies in the eighteenth century. All roads lead back to Jean-Jacques Rousseau. One of the lecturers on the Diploma of Education courses at Cambridge made us write down the first sentence of Rousseau's treatise on education, called *Émile* and published in 1762: 'Everything is good as it comes from the hands of the Author of Nature (Rousseau's phrase is *'l'auteur des choses'*); but everything degenerates in the hands of man.' In other words, a child is born innocent and only corrupted by society.

Rousseau stands the doctrine of original sin on its head. If you believe a child is born sinful, education, whether by school or by parents, is a process of forcing into the child – by repetition, by fear – what the adult world has decided the child must learn. The child is made to accommodate himself to the school, not vice-versa. He is not really a child at all, just

25

a young adult. In sixteenth- and seventeenth-century family portraits the children are present but they might as well be adult dwarfs. They are portrayed and dressed as small-scale adults. They would have been educated as small-scale adults too.

Rousseau rejected this view. In its place he 'invented' childhood. A child, he argued, moved towards adulthood through a number of distinct stages, at each of which the child is capable of organizing the information he receives in his own way. The information does not have to be rammed down his throat. So at the early stage – which Rousseau decided was from the cradle to the age of twelve – the child learns primarily through the senses and by making his own discoveries: it is only later that he becomes capable of intellectual understanding and analytical reasoning. Whatever the stage, Rousseau places great emphasis on telling the child as little as possible and encouraging him to find things out for himself.

It is easy to point out that Rousseau's ideas on education are sometimes impracticable and sometimes just silly. The existence of God, for example, is not to be revealed to Émile until he is eighteen because only then is he capable of grasping the abstract concept. But such criticisms have done nothing to lessen Rousseau's influence. It is the *spirit* of his educational philosophy, not the detail, that matters. The idea that education should be child-centred, that it should take account of the progressive stages in a child's development (which is the origin of the phrase 'progressive education', though it is now used in the general sense of being 'on the side of progress'), and that it should encourage the child to discover rather than be told, have all exerted a powerful influence on western education.

In the Pantheon in Paris, the tombs of Rousseau and Voltaire face one another. Educationalists who worship at Rousseau's shrine like to portray him as Voltaire's equal in the overthrow of superstition, prejudice and cruelty. They believe that child-centred education is on a par with religious toleration as a characteristic of a civilized society. It is worth pointing out, therefore, that the view of education that Rousseau overthrew had its origins not in religious bigotry but in the work of the humanist educators of the Renaissance, who had no romantic sentiments about the natural goodness of the child. The full impact of Rousseau's ideas was not felt by British education for two hundred years. There were progressive schools long before that but they remained on the fringe, exerting little influence on the mainstream. It was the prevailing mood of liberalization in the 1960s that provided the platform for child-centred education to take off in Britain.

Because it was so much at one with the spirit of the times, progressive education was hard to resist. People who should have known better found themselves cheering the revolution. But very few independent schools allowed progressive ideas to take root. Their young headteachers (including myself) flirted with progressive theories but had no intention of introducing the practice, except in modified form. The power of tradition, the steadying influence of long-established members of staff and the imperatives of the market place were an effective brake on ambitious heads and ill-considered reforms. Exams had to be passed, matches had to be won. What the independent schools were successful in doing was in using progressive ideas to modernize their curriculum and teaching methods and to abolish some of the sillier aspects of public school convention and discipline. When the counter-revolution was in full swing, this caution turned out to have been a good investment. The principal reason why the independent schools are flourishing today is that they managed to modernize themselves without abandoning the spirit and style of traditional education.

The state sector would not have accepted progressive ideas

so uncritically if it had not been in the process of going comprehensive. The grammar schools, like the independent schools, would have adopted a more cautious approach. But when a grammar school was forced into marriage with two secondary modern schools, the grammar-school tradition was soon forgotten and long-established teachers found themselves in a minority. By the late Sixties, progressive ideas of child-centred education had already taken hold in the primary sector. Comprehensive schools made it easier for them to take hold in the secondary sector as well.

Though the independent schools had not been enthusiastic about progressive ideas, neither had they been openly critical. As the Sixties drew to a close, there was a remarkable consensus of support of both comprehensive schools and progressive ideas in education. That consensus was broken in the spring of 1969.

The counter-revolution

The signal for the start of the counter-revolution was the publication in 1969 of the first Black Paper, a collection of essays challenging the fashionable consensus. 'It is our belief', wrote the editors, 'that disastrous mistakes are being made in modern education and that an urgent reappraisal is required of the assumptions on which "progressive" ideas, now in the ascendant, are based.'

The effect was dramatic. No one had dared to question the doctrine of the progressive faith. There was a touch of hysteria in the reaction of the high priests. Ted Short, Labour's Education Secretary at the time, said the publication of the Black Paper was 'one of the blackest days for education in the past 100 years'. The press took a similar view. The *New Statesman* called the authors 'a decrepit bunch of educational Powellites'. Less predictably, London's *Evening Standard*, which is today a consistent critic of progressive education, described the Black Paper as 'a trivial document by a bunch of elderly reactionaries'. The Black Paper thrived on abuse. A second Black Paper was published in the same year and a third in 1970. Sales of the first three Black Papers passed 80,000. A fourth and fifth Black Paper appeared in 1975 and 1976. By then the progressive consensus had been well and truly broken and the counter-revolution had acquired its own momentum.

The theme of all the Black Papers was to question every assumption on which progressive education and comprehensive schooling were based. The virtues of the grammar school, of traditional methods of teaching, and of the independent school were forcefully argued. The moving spirits in the 'bunch of elderly reactionaries' were the not-so-elderly Dr Rhodes Boyson and Professor Brian Cox. Boyson was headmaster of a north London comprehensive, Highbury Grove, where he had succeeded in retaining the ethos and the trappings of a grammar school. In 1974, he became a Conservative MP and listed among his recreations in *Who's Who* 'inciting the millenialistic Left in education'. His pugnacious, populist style gave the counter-revolution an excellent champion in the public forum and his long experience in the trenches of state education gave the counter-revolution a credibility it might otherwise have lacked. When I came to know Boyson in the Seventies, I found him a friendly, open, and sincere man and I respected him as someone who, unlike myself, had had the courage to speak out against the flaws in progressive education from the start.

The ideological thrust of the counter-revolution was provided by Brian Cox. Cox was Professor of English at Manchester University and like Boyson a state-school boy from a humble home who had made good. In the early days, the counter-revolution received little support from the independent schools or from their former pupils. A notable exception was Tom Howarth, the High Master of St Paul's School, whose own attack on progressive education, *Culture, Anarchy and the Public Schools*, was published in the same year as the first Black Paper.

Those who had used the grammar schools as a ladder of opportunity felt most keenly that comprehensive schools and progressive education were betraying the working class. They resented the way in which the middle classes, who sent their children to independent schools, appeared to be acquiescing in an egalitarian revolution that hit the bright working-class child hardest of all. Their hand was strengthened by the Conservative victory in the general election of 1970. The new Secretary of State for Education was Margaret Thatcher, a grammar-school girl from a modest home who had made good.

Margaret Thatcher left no one in any doubt where her sympathies lay. She could not stop the comprehensive bandwagon but she could and did slow it down. Within days she had withdrawn Crosland's 1965 Circular and replaced it with one of her own, giving local authorities the freedom to retain selective schools if they wished to do so. She was willing to approve schemes for 'going comprehensive', even when a local grammar school was excluded from the scheme. By 1974, when Labour returned to power, half the comprehensive schools in the country still had a grammar school in the vicinity. Margaret Thatcher had won the first political victory for the counter-revolution.

Under the Conservatives, the social revolution had slowed down. So had the comprehensive bandwagon. But neither had stopped. The spread of progressive ideas in education through the state sector had hardly been affected by Margaret Thatcher's instinctive hostility. The Black Papers had set the counter-revolution in motion but very few people in the education establishment took them very seriously. The teachers' unions, the school inspectors, the training colleges and the university departments of education, all to a greater or lesser degree, made the mistake of dismissing the ideas put forward by the Black Papers as reactionary and unimportant. With characteristic arrogance, they failed to recognize that the doubts expressed in the Black Papers were also being expressed by many parents and employers. It took a Labour Prime Minister, James Callaghan, to make the educationists accept that not everyone was convinced that the new utopia of comprehensive schools and progressive teaching methods was working well.

Callaghan's speech at Ruskin College, Oxford, in 1976 has acquired a reputation as a turning-point in the history of post-war education that it does not deserve. From the point of view of the counter-revolution, the speech was less important than the setting-up of the Centre for Policy Studies by Margaret Thatcher and Keith Joseph the previous year.

The Centre was a Conservative think-tank to review all aspects of party policy in the wake of the electoral defeat in 1974. Its education study group was headed by Caroline Cox (no relation of Brian Cox) and John Marks, both of whom contributed to the later Black Papers. While Callaghan's speech launched the much publicized Great Debate on education, the Centre quietly got on with the business of transforming the counter-revolution into a set of radical policies that were intended to destroy the left-wing consensus in education once and for all. A comparison of the questions Callaghan asked in public with the more radical questions Cox and Marks were asking in private gives a valuable insight into how we got to where we are.

Callaghan wanted to know why some children left school without basic skills in literacy and numeracy; why so few pupils, particularly girls, chose science and engineering, and why students in universities and polytechnics seldom wanted to go into industry. By way of an answer to the first question, he expressed a preference for a basic curriculum that did not sacrifice a good grounding in essential subjects for the doubtful benefits of diversity on the timetable. Callaghan was probably more in sympathy with the writers of the Black Papers than he was with the middle-class idealists who advocated comprehensive schools and progressive teaching methods. He had seen how many doors education could unlock for working-class children and he feared that newfangled teaching methods might rob these children of the opportunity to better themselves. But his Ruskin speech is only by implication critical of the status quo. He wants to know why the education system is not working as well as it should. What he does not question is whether the system itself ought to be changed.

The Centre for Policy Studies was asking more fundamental questions: how do you make schools more accountable to parents? How do you give parents an effective choice of schools? It was this emphasis on the role of parents that distinguished the Centre's radical approach from Callaghan's genuine but conservatively framed criticisms. Callaghan still believed that education was a matter for teachers (though he was annoyed when the *Times Educational Supplement*, the teachers' trade paper, questioned his competence to speak about education). The Centre thought that teachers could not be trusted to dictate the contents and methods of education. 'Teachers', Callaghan said at Ruskin, 'must carry parents with them.' But the Centre wanted to change the balance of power so that in future it would be the parents who would call the tune.

The Great Debate that followed Callaghan's speech was stage-managed by the Department of Education and Science. The Department, like the Centre for Policy Studies, wanted to reduce the power of teachers. But whereas the Centre wanted more power for parents, the Department wanted more power for itself. Parent power was not on the agenda in 1977, but its time would come.

What the Department wanted to see publicly debated was the connection between education and the economy, and the responsibility of schools to give pupils the skills they needed to find employment. So in 1977, the pattern of conflict in education became more complex. The swing to comprehensive schools had accelerated with Labour in power again and a new Secretary of State, Shirley Williams, taking steps to eliminate the remaining grammar schools. The struggle between the traditionalists and the progressives continued to go the latters' way despite the Black Papers and the criticisms implicit in Callaghan's speech.

In public, the counter-revolution still had few supporters. Many who were pleased to see the values of traditional education championed, nevertheless kept their views to themselves, because they thought it unlikely that the traditionalists would ever regain the initiative. Meanwhile the Centre for Policy Studies was working on a radical programme that, ten years later, would become the basis of the most important education act since 1944.

While the counter-revolutionaries and progressives slugged it out, the Department of Education and Science saw an opportunity to extend its control over the education system, particularly over the curriculum. The Department recognized and used a growing public unease at the dangerous discontinuity between what was taught in school and what were regarded as the realities of economic life. It is here that a new struggle, between 'utilitarians' and 'purists', between those who supported and those who opposed greater central control of education, had its origins.

It was at this point that I was elected chairman of the Headmasters Conference, which represented the leading independent schools. The independent schools had not been formally invited to take part in the Great Debate but I thought it was a mistake for the schools to remain silent on the issues that it raised.

From the start, the issue that attracted me most was that of central direction of the curriculum. I hesitated to attack progressive education; I could see its failings, but like most heads of independent schools, I was reluctant to expose them. I had no such hesitation in saying that I was in favour of the central government having more power to tell schools what they should teach. I have not suddenly become a utilitarian in writing this book. On 3 February 1977, just before the Great Debate was formally launched, I wrote a feature article in *The Times*, arguing the case for the central government, on behalf of society, to dictate the curriculum. 'For too long', I wrote, a little bombastically, 'the teachers and education theorists have claimed the right to tell the nation what the children shall learn.' A few weeks later I made the same point in a two-hour television discussion on education, but mine was an isolated voice. 'The debate showed a surprising amount of agreement between Mrs Williams and her opposition shadow, Mr Norman St John Stevas,' *The Times* reported. 'Both rejected the idea of a common core curriculum imposed on schools by central government . . .'

At the Annual Meeting of the Headmasters Conference that year I had an opportunity to stake out my position on a wider range of issues. I told my colleagues that they must accept greater central direction of the curriculum. Almost without exception they rejected it. Reports of the speech drew condemnation from a wider circle. The Left invoked the memory of Hitler and called me a Fascist. The Right thought the idea of central control of the curriculum was dangerously socialist.

I mention my own involvement in the Great Debate not

because my interventions had any effect on the outcome but because it helps to explain my stance throughout this book. I was convinced then and have remained so since that one of the most obvious lessons of history is that only the most powerful and prosperous countries can afford to let education go its own way; and that other nations have to use the education system to achieve national (usually economic or military) goals. This utilitarian view of education is most dominant at times when nations are trying to catch up with other states or to adjust to a new ideology or to come to terms with a fundamentally altered position in the world. France at the time of the Revolution and under Napoleon, Prussia after its crushing defeat by Napoleon at Jena in 1806, Japan in the latter part of the nineteenth century, are examples that come to mind, to which should be added post-1945 Britain whose imperial and economic power had by then been critically undermined.

I still find it extraordinary that as late as 1977, when Britain's relative economic decline was plain for all to see, both major political parties were firmly opposed to the idea of greater central government direction of education. It is a reminder of the extent to which politicians focus on short-term political goals and find it difficult to see the larger historical and international context.

In 1977 the Department of Education and Science was not so blind to the need to make education more accountable to the economy. The Department did not get its way at this point but it had put down a marker for the future. Sooner or later the politicians would have to come to terms with the connection between do-as-you-please education and economic decline. Meanwhile the Great Debate petered out. Politicians and educationalists had used it to ride their own hobby horses and had not asked the vital question of what British education was *for*. The Labour Government had no interest in radical reform, certainly not in any change in the traditional balance of power between the education service and the central government. Shirley Williams was opposed to the idea of a core curriculum imposed by the state and had only included it in the Debate at Callaghan's insistence. Callaghan did not press the issue and within two years was out of office. His Ruskin speech which seemed to mark a partial acceptance of the need for a counter-revolution turned out to be a nine-days' wonder.

The counter-revolution in full swing

The Conservative victory in the general election of 1979 did not suddenly make the counter-revolution popular. But it gave the Centre for Policy Studies, with its radical proposals for the reform of education, direct access to power. The influence of the so-called New Right in education was all the greater because the Prime Minister, Margaret Thatcher, was in sympathy with its views. Yet the radical programme did not become law until the Education Act of 1988. It required Mrs Thatcher to win three elections in a row before she and her party were ready to put into practice the ideas that the counter-revolutionaries had nurtured for so long.

There were various reasons for this delay. The most obvious was that educational reform, however dear to the Prime Minister's heart, was not the government's priority. The appointment of Mark Carlisle as Secretary of State for Education and Science suggests that Mrs Thatcher made a conscious decision to postpone the counter-revolution. Carlisle was an able, middle-of-the-road Tory, but he had neither the political clout nor the ideological conviction to lead the counter-attack against progressive education and the comprehensive schools.

Another reason for the delay was that public opinion was not yet ready to accept such radical ideas as a national curriculum and the need to give parents not teachers the whip-hand in schools. Despite apparent popular interest, education was not a major issue in the elections of 1979 and 1983. As far as the counter-revolution was concerned, the first two Thatcher governments were marked not by reform but by increasing public criticism of the standards in state schools. This was no formal public debate stage-managed by the Department of Education and Science. It was popular and spontaneous and fanned by the media. All of a sudden – it seemed – no one had a good word to say for the state sector of education. Teacher-bashing became a popular sport. Public criticism increased when the teachers' unions and the left wing in education were too complacent or stupid to recognize that the popular dissatisfaction was real, not a creation of the Tory press. Left-wing local education authorities played into Tory hands by their provocative obsession with anti-racist policies. The teachers' unions made a similar mistake, alienating public sympathy by disrupting schools in support of pay claims. By the mid-1980s the climate of opinion had changed to such a degree that ideas that only recently had been unthinkable – the right of schools to opt out of local authority control is a good example – had become practical politics.

There is no mystery about why public disquiet about state schools should become so much more pronounced at this time. The disquiet had been there for many years under the surface; now that there was a Prime Minister who, unlike Callaghan, was explicit in her dislike of progressive education and comprehensive schools, there was no longer any need for people who shared her views to remain silent. Mrs Thatcher did not have to impose a climate of opinion favourable to the counter-revolution; all she had to do was to release the parental and public anxiety that was already there.

By the mid-1980s the time had come for the government's long-awaited counter-attack against progressive education and against the educational establishment that had called the tune for so long. The Secretary of State was Sir Keith Joseph, a good intelligence officer but not the man to take command of the operation. In May 1986 Joseph resigned and was replaced by Kenneth Baker, who, though less familiar with the issues and less committed perhaps to the right-wing ideology, nevertheless had the stature, the political astuteness, and the ambition to lead the campaign.

The result was the Education Reform Act of 1988. The character of the Act reflected the two principal forces that had brought it into being: the Department's determination that central government should take control of the curriculum, and the counter-revolutionaries' determination to take education out of the hands of the producers so that the consumers could reverse once and for all the progressive and left-wing trends that had run unchecked for a quarter of a century.

There were really two Acts (three, including the sections dealing with the universities with which we are not concerned). The first 'Act' established the national curriculum and the system of the national tests to check the effectiveness of its operation. The second 'Act' introduced the counter-revolutionary ideas, most of which had their origin in the Centre for Policy Studies. These included the right of schools to opt out of their local authority control, the delegation of financial powers to governing bodies and headteachers, the removal of local authority limits on the numbers that a school could admit, and the provision of a legal framework for setting up independent City Technology Colleges.

As I shall refer to these provisions of the Act at various stages in my argument, it might be helpful if I described them in greater detail.

1 The national curriculum requires all state schools to teach English, maths, science, history, geography, technology,

music, art, and physical education to pupils of all ages, and a modern foreign language to pupils aged 11 to 16. English, maths, and science are the 'core' subjects, the remainder being described as 'foundation' subjects, the practical effect of this distinction being that the 'core' subjects will have more periods allotted to them on the timetable. It is envisaged that the compulsory subjects will occupy 70% of the timetable, leaving 30% for optional subjects, though these percentages will vary at different ages. The Secretary of State will prescribe the programme of study in each of the compulsory subjects as well as the targets that children will be expected to reach at the ages of 7, 11, 14, and 16. He will also establish a system of national tests at these ages to check on the children's progress. Parents will see the test results for their own children; school and local authority area results will be made public.

The national curriculum will be introduced from September 1989. Religious education is not part of the national curriculum, but the Act requires state schools to provide it for all pupils nevertheless.

2   Schools with more than 300 pupils will be able to opt out of local authority control if a majority of parents vote in favour. If fewer than 50% of the parents take part in the ballot, a second ballot will be held within 14 days the result of which will be binding irrespective of the parental turn-out. The school's decision to opt out must be confirmed by the Secretary of State but once that confirmation has been given the decision is irreversible. Opting-out schools will be called 'grant maintained schools'. They will be funded by central government on the same financial basis as schools that remain in local authority control. The Act does not make clear whether the grant maintained schools will be allowed to change their character by – for example – having a selective rather than a comprehensive intake.

3   All schools with more than 200 pupils will have financial powers delegated to them. They will receive a budget from the local authority which they will be free to spend as they wish. The budget will cover all running costs, including staff salaries. Although teachers will, in theory, continue to be employed by the local authority, in practice it will be the school's governing body that has the power to 'hire and fire'.

4   All schools will be able to admit as many pupils as they have space for. Local authority limits to ensure that the less popular schools receive their fair share of pupils will now be illegal.

5   The Secretary of State is allowed to enter into agreement with 'any person' to establish a City Technology College for 11- to 19-year-olds. The College may not charge fees (it will be funded direct from Whitehall), must be in an urban area, admit pupils of 'different abilities' and provide a curriculum with an emphasis on science and technology.

There are other provisions in the Act that affect schools but these are the ones that matter. The authors of the Act see it as a major break with Britain's past educational practice and as such a response to the needs of Britain's changed role in the world. How far the Act does go to meet those needs and how far it fails to do so will – I hope – become clear as the argument in this book develops.

2

WHAT SHOULD BE THE AIMS
OF EDUCATION?

A striking feature of British education is a reluctance on every-one's part to define what the aims of the education should be. The Butler Act offered pious platitudes about contributing to the spiritual, moral, mental and physical development of the community. The Baker Act is only marginally more down-to-earth when it adds that pupils should be prepared 'for the opportunities, responsibilities and experiences of adult life'.

In the context of Britain's economic and social problems this reluctance looks like a sin of omission. What is the point of spending £18 billion a year on education if you are not clear what education is for?

The needs of the individual or the needs of the state?

There is no such thing as education for its own sake. All educa-tion has a purpose. It is as well to establish this at the outset because there are people – particularly in academic life and particularly in Britain – who believe that if only the state can be prevented from imposing its own goals, education will be innocent of any attempt to fashion, mould or indoctrinate the pupils. But teaching is always directed towards a specific end, otherwise there would be no point in doing it.

The conflict is not between education for its own sake and education in the service of the state. It is between education that is being directed towards the interests of the individual and education in which the priority is the interests of the state. The former represents the liberal tradition of education and it is with this tradition that I wish to start.

When education is for the benefit of the individual, the aim is usually expressed in very general terms, such as 'developing the whole personality'. The trouble with such fine phrases is to know exactly what they mean. Education is awash with generalities. Do the fine phrases mean anything or are they merely verbal conjuring tricks that create the illusion of noble purposes? More often than not they are a form of educational hype. If you press headmasters and headmistresses to say what they mean by 'developing the whole personality', they will answer that their school offers a wide range of out-of-school activities and that the aims of the school are not narrowly academic. The idea of an all-round education is laudable enough but if that is what is meant by developing the whole personality, then the phrase is far too high-sounding for what is being attempted.

While educationalists use high-sounding phrases to describe what they are doing for the individual child, parents are more down-to-earth. They do not see the aims of education in philosophical terms. They want their child to learn to read, write, and do mathematics with appropriate skill, to learn the discipline of work and behaviour, to be encouraged to develop any talents he or she has and to obtain whatever qualification is needed to make a start in the adult world.

It is natural that educationalists should emphasize the more philosophical and parents the more down-to-earth aims of education. Teachers wish to be seen as more than mere instructors. Parents have dreams too, but uppermost in their mind is the fear that if their child does not learn the basics now, he or she will have missed the boat for ever.

Whether the aim is expressed in idealistic or practical terms, it is the interests of the individual, not the interests of the state, that provide the inspiration. Educationalists and parents agree that the aim is to enable children to mature in such a way that they may have – to coin a phrase – 'life in all its fullness', not to fit them into an economic plan or any other plan that the state may wish to impose. (I should make it clear that when I speak of the 'state' I mean the central government, whether totalitarian or democratic, as distinct from 'society' which is the people not the government.)

This view of the aims of education – 'liberal', 'democratic', 'humane', call it what you will – is most strongly held in those English-speaking countries that have a traditional dislike of centralized power. Countries that have tended to favour strong central authority, such as France, Russia or Japan, while not rejecting the claims of the individual, are more inclined to interpret the aims of education in terms of conformity, and the interests of the state. Many developing countries would also argue that a liberal education emphasizing individual interests is not appropriate to a society that needs specific skills. One of the underlying questions in the current debate on education in the United Kingdom, is whether the loss of world-power status makes Britain a developing country that needs to abandon its decentralized and liberal tradition in education.

The liberal tradition of education is so well-established in Britain that we tend to think that its roots must be in the very distant past. But for centuries education in this country was controlled by the Catholic Church. When, in the sixteenth century, Henry VIII seized control of the Church for himself he was no less determined to dictate the aims of education. In his own words, children were to be 'brought up under one absolute and uniform sort of learning'.

What we have inherited as the liberal tradition, developed

gradually as the power and influence of the Established Church receded in education and was not replaced by state control. In this power vacuum the liberal tradition flourished. As long as the central government had no specific demands of the education system, the aims of education in Britain could be focused on the interests of the individual.

The liberal tradition was alive and well when I became headmaster of Westminster in 1970. Although the British by that time were by no means unaware of the extent of their industrial and economic decline, any attempt to mobilize the education system in the cause of industrial and economic regeneration would have met with fierce opposition in parliament and in the country. I would have opposed such an attempt myself. My Nonconformist background and education predisposed me to favour the liberal approach to education that Westminster exemplified. The independence of mind that seems to be so deeply inbedded in the Westminster tradition was the quality that I most wanted to encourage in my pupils. When prospective parents asked me what my educational aims were – and they did often – I answered that I wanted to encourage the boys and girls to think for themselves, to be independent in their judgements, to have the courage and intelligence to make up their own minds on issues and to stick to their opinions unless the evidence clearly showed them that they were wrong, in which case they should be open-minded enough to admit their error. To me, prejudice and bigotry were the two great enemies against which a good education must equip its pupils to fight.

My view of what education was for was in the mainstream of the British liberal tradition. At Westminster, I think it worked; the school did produce individuals of independent mind, not so much because that was the aim of any one headmaster, but because the ideal was so well-established that it was handed on from generation to generation of teachers and pupils and because parents who sympathized with the ideal chose Westminster for their children. How strong this tradition was is illustrated by a story of a seventeenth-century headmaster of Westminster, Dr Richard Busby. Busby's Royalist sympathies made him regret that one of his favourite pupils, Philip Henry, had become a Nonconformist. 'Child what made thee a Nonconformist?' Busby asked. 'Truly, sir', was the reply, 'you made me one, for you taught me those things that hindered me from conforming.'

To teach your pupils those things that hinder them from conforming was what I came to believe was the principal aim of a liberal education. But I did not deceive myself that I pursued this aim solely in the interests of the individual. I also believed that the sort of education Westminster offered was in the interests of society, particularly a democratic society. The less prejudiced and bigoted the citizens the more enlightened the society would be and the safer its democratic tradition. In this sense, I was using education in just the same way as, for example, the French Revolutionaries, who aimed to build an ideal society by insisting that schools taught their pupils republican virtues.

Just as there is no such thing as education for its own sake, so there is also no such thing as education that is solely in the interests of the individual. The aims of education cannot, after all, be divided into two clear categories: education for the sake of the individual and education for the sake of society or state. Whatever the style and content of an education system, the intention is that both the individual and society will benefit. It is a question of which is given the priority, of where the emphasis is laid. The aims of education can best be understood as a spectrum with the liberal goal of independence of mind at one end and the most totalitarian suppression of individual thought at the other. Britain's problem in the late Eighties is to decide how far along the spectrum it is prepared to move from its liberal education tradition towards an accommodation with the interests of the state.

One of the difficulties of even contemplating such a move is that teachers regard the spectrum as a slippery slope on which it is impossible to find a foothold. They fear that once the central government gets in on the act it will inevitably exert greater and greater control over what is taught, and they seem to be unaware that other countries have found it possible to comprehend within one education system the interests of the individual and the interests, whether these are economic or social, of the central government. It is this ignorance, sometimes amounting to xenophobia, that I would like to dispel.

At the liberal end of the spectrum, I would place the ideal expressed by the British war-time government in 1943. In its White Paper, *Educational Reconstruction*, the purpose of post-war educational reform would be:

> to secure for children a happier childhood and a better start in life; to ensure a fuller measure of education and opportunity for young people and to provide means for all of developing the various talents with which they are endowed and so enriching the inheritance of the country whose citizens they are.

The individual comes first. The enriching of society is not forgotten but it is an afterthought. This idea has guided British education for forty years. Further along the spectrum the interests of society are more central. This definition of the aims of education comes from an educational foundation in contemporary USA:

> Its central purpose is to enable students to function reasonably in society i.e. to have proper discrimination in the realm of ideas and proper judgement in the world of action.

That seems to coincide with my concept of independence of mind, but already the interests of the individual are being linked to the need of a democratic society to have citizens who act reasonably. The desire to produce citizens who act reasonably echoes the aims of the French Revolutionaries just as much as it does the British liberal tradition.

If I frequently cite the French Revolution, it is because the men and women who participated in it were acutely aware of the need to define their educational aims. Their opportunity to start afresh, to base an educational system on ideals rather than on tradition, makes their attempts to balance the interests of the individual and the interests of the state especially interesting. The more extreme revolutionaries swung quickly to the totalitarian end of the spectrum. 'I too am a father', said Danton in 1793, 'but my son does not belong to me. He belongs to the Republic. It is for her to decide what he ought to do to serve her well.' That is the voice of totalitarian democracy and it produced a scheme to send all children to state boarding schools at the age of five to be indoctrinated with republican and revolutionary ideals.

Earlier in the Revolution the more liberal Condorcet put before the Assembly a plan for national education that was a genuine attempt to reconcile the interests of the individual and of the state:

> To afford all members of the human race the means of providing for their needs, of securing their welfare, of recognizing and exercizing their rights, of understanding and fulfilling their duties; to assure for everyone opportunities of perfecting their skill and rendering themselves capable of the social duties to which they have a right to be called; to develop to the utmost the talents with which nature has endowed them and in so doing, to establish among all citizens a true equality and

47

thus make the political equality realized by law – this should be the primary aim of a national system of education . . .

That is the voice of liberal democracy, but while it has much in common with the 1943 British definition it is much more emphatic on the need of society to educate young people to recognize their social duties.

Condorcet's approach to the purpose of education is interesting from another point of view. He argued that individual happiness and economic prosperity would *both* increase if his definition of the purpose of education was adopted. He believed that prosperity as well as true equality would be the result of developing to the utmost the talents of all citizens. Far from there being a conflict between the liberal tradition and the economic needs of the state, they coincide. The French Revolutionaries also faced a social problem that is relevant to modern Britain. France was divided, not only politically but by language and custom. The Revolutionary planners saw education as a unifying force. The French children would be united by a common curriculum, above all by a common language. 'La langue d'un peuple libre doit être une et la même pour tous', Barère told the Convention in 1794. What the revolutionaries were aiming to achieve was that same social cohesion that Mr Kenneth Baker argues will be one of the benefits of a national curriculum.

As we move across the spectrum, the problem of reconciling the interests of the individual and the interests of the state becomes more difficult to solve. The classic confrontation between these two poles of the educational idea occurred in 1945 when the United States defeated and occupied Japan. The USA, a country whose tradition since its creation had been of liberal education, had to impose a new system on a society in which education had latterly been rigorously dedicated to the service of the state. The outcome of this clash between the two traditions is an education system that is widely regarded as one of the most effective in the world today.

The Japanese education system had been created in the late nineteenth century. For nearly three hunded years Japan's rulers had followed an extreme isolationist policy. In the mid-nineteenth century the country was still cut off from the industrialization of the West. A desire to catch up industrially and a fear of Western military technology prompted a group of young upper-class samurai to overthrow the isolationist regime in 1868, and the Meiji era began. The new rulers quickly understood that modernization depended on taking control of education. They also understood that economic prosperity required a well-educated population: 'There shall in future be no community with an illiterate family nor a family with an illiterate person.'

The key figure in the creation of a centralized education system was the Minister of Education between 1885 and 1889, Mori Arinori. He made no bones about the aims: 'Education is not for the sake of the student but for the sake of the state.' What that meant in practice was that the central government ensured that the schools promoted national unity, produced a core of competent technicians, and trained an elite who would be committed to national goals. To object that such aims were bad because they were nationalistic and subordinated the individual to the needs of the state is to miss the point. Japan had to catch up with the West: in these circumstances liberal educational ideals had to take second place. The late nineteenth-century leaders of Japan were not ideologically totalitarian. They were practical men who believed that the nation's survival depended on the state's direction of education. Their ideas were corrupted by the Japanese militarists of the twentieth century, and it was the resulting system that the Americans tried to convert into a democratic, egalitarian system after 1945. The United States Education Mission to Japan laid down the new philosophy. Education must recognize 'the worth and dignity of the individual' and prepare the individual 'to become a responsible and co-operating member of society'. These ideals were enshrined in the Mission's First Fundamental Law of Education: the aims of Japan's post-war education system echoed the liberal tradition of the English-speaking world and the need for social responsibility that had characterized the educational schemes of the early French Revolutionaries such as Condorcet:

> Education shall aim at the full development of personality striving for the rearing of the people, sound in mind and body, who shall love truth and justice, esteem individual value, respect labour and have a deep sense of responsibility and be imbued with an independent spirit, as builders of a peaceful state and society.

The United States saw the new educational philosophy as a safeguard against a resurgence of Japanese militarism. So it proved to be. But it also laid the foundation for Japan's resurgence as a great economic power. The combination of the Western liberal tradition and the tradition of centralized education inherited from Mori Arinori, produced an education system ideally suited to the needs of an economy based on the efficient exploitation of new and sophisticated technology. By one of those ironies in which history abounds, the Americans had given the Japanese the means to reverse in economic terms, the military defeat of 1945.

What the Japanese succeeded in doing was to keep the control of curriculum in the hands of the central government while bowing to the American policy of introducing democratic features, such as the first Japanese teachers' union. When the Americans insisted that the new education should be egalitarian not elitist, the Japanese seized the opportunity to make high quality education available to all children, boys and girls. The individual counts for more in today's Japanese education system than he did under Mori Arinori, but the system is no less closely aligned with the state's economic goals than it was a hundred years ago.

The success of Japan's education system (a topic I shall return to in later chapters) also demonstrates that you do not have to be a totalitarian regime to harness the education system successfully in the national interest. The liberals argue that once you allow the state to control the curriculum, you will be in Nazi Germany before you realize what has happened. When Prime Minister Callaghan spoke in favour of a common core curriculum in 1977, the general secretary of the National Association of Head Teachers said, 'I was teaching in Nazi Germany in the 'thirties and saw what happened where the curriculum was nationally controlled.' Like so many educationalists, he believed that any control of the curriculum was tantamount to totalitarianism.

It is central to my argument that these instinctive antipathies are misguided; a national curriculum, imposed by central government, need not be incompatible with an education that aims to meet the needs of the individual. The safeguard is democracy itself. It is only when the government is undemocratic that the individual's interests are subordinated to the interests of the state.

The Soviet Union provides a good example of an education system that subordinates the interests of the individual to the interests of the state. The idea of schooling as something to broaden the mind and develop personality is alien not only to the Soviet tradition but to the Russian tradition too. When Peter the Great, who was Tsar at the beginning of the eighteenth century, laid the foundations of state (as distinct from church) education in Russia, he acted from the same motives as the young samurai who took power in Japan at the end of the nineteenth century. Russia had to be modernized, particularly in technology and industry, in order to catch up with the West. In the schools Peter established, the emphasis was on teaching the practical skills that the state needed. When the Bolsheviks seized power in 1917, they took a similarly utilitarian view of the aims of education. Once again Russia had fallen behind industrially. Schools must therefore be 'polytechnized', an unattractive word which means to make the school curriculum reflect the manual skills that industry needs. Neither this nor subsequent drives to 'polytechnize' schools was wholly successful (even in Russia teachers resisted such obvious attempts to marry the education system and industry) but the underlying philosophy remains the same today: education is not for the sake of the student but for the sake of the state. The state needs manual workers and good communists: the schools' job is to provide both. The ideological and economic goals of Soviet education were well expressed by Nikita Khrushchev in 1958:

all children who enter school must be trained for useful labour and participation in the construction of a communist society ... The Soviet school is required to produce well-rounded people who know their school subjects well but who are at the same time capable of useful labour; it must develop in young people an urge to be useful to society and participate actively in the production of the wealth which society needs.

The justification for this approach to education is simple. The first duty of the state is to ensure the security of the society it serves. If that requires the development of particular skills or particular types of citizen, the education system must be geared accordingly. Education that puts the individual first is a luxury that only very secure nations can afford. State-directed education is the norm in many more countries than is an education where the interests of the individual come first.

Until recently, Britain believed that it could afford to give the needs of the individual the priority. British education was liberal in philosophy and decentralized in organization. This belief has now been undermined, above all by the radical change in Britain's role and status. Britain is no longer a world power, no longer an industrial leader, no longer a society with a sense of cultural unity.

These changes have not occurred overnight but it is only in the 1980s that the British people have realized that they can no longer afford to let schools go their own way and that some accommodation has to be made with the need for education to make its contribution to the solving of economic and social problems.

What should be the aims of education in contemporary Britain?

If I had been asked this question twenty years ago, I should have answered in terms of my interpretation of the liberal tradition. Any suggestion that the state should impose its own goals on education would have been as alien to me as the liberal tradition would have been to the Soviets. Yet, as I have explained, by 1977 I had become convinced of the need for a national curriculum and for greater centralization of power in the education system. Two factors led me to abandon the strict liberal tradition.

In the first place, I was won over by the arguments put forward in the 1970s, notably by the historian Corelli Barnett, that there was a direct connection between the failings of the education system and Britain's economic and industrial decline. Secondly, I was persuaded that the new religious and cultural diversity of the British population required the central government to make sure that schools did not fail to pass on to all children the common cultural heritage of Britain, particularly in language and history.

So much has been written about education's responsibility for Britain's industrial decline that it should be sufficient here to summarize the main steps in the argument.

British education developed piecemeal. There never was a central or national idea of what education was for. Political philosophers such as John Locke and Jeremy Bentham theorized about the purpose of education but it was not a question that interested the country as a whole. To many people in Britain it seemed a pretentious and abstract question. Education was not for anything in particular; it was a rite of passage that with luck would see the pupil through the turmoil of adolescence and deliver him to adulthood with some of the trappings of a gentleman. The curriculum remained fundamentally the same for centuries, partly because the study of Latin and Greek was thought to be worthwhile in itself but partly, too, because the ancient languages could not be said to possess any utilitarian value. If new subjects tried to muscle in they were given short shrift. At Cambridge University at the end of the nineteenth century, the dons thought that any subject that could be turned to the benefit of business should not be given university recognition. French and German could not be instruments of humane learning because they were useful in international trade. When economic rivalry with Germany prompted a proposal that German should be studied, the classicists denounced the ideas as utilitarian.

The study of the classics was acceptable because although it might develop qualities of mind it was in other respects pointless. When Harold Macmillan went up to Oxford just before

the First World War, his classics tutor at Balliol told the new
undergraduates:

> Nothing that you will learn on the course of studies will
> be the slightest use to you in after life, save only this, that
> if you work hard and diligently you should be able to
> detect when a man is talking rot and in my view that is
> the main if not the sole purpose of education.

Whatever the virtues of this approach to education, its anti-
utilitarian and anti-industrial bias appears in retrospect
like the foolish pride of an aristocratic class who refuse to
recognize that their privileged world is doomed. Yet the bias
survived well into the second half of the twentieth century.
When I suggested to the head of classics at Westminster in
the 1970s that he should publish the well-paid jobs that his
scholars had secured, he refused to do so on the grounds
that it would imply that the study of classics had a utilitarian
purpose. Even more recently, the proposal to introduce a
national curriculum was attacked because it was based on 'too
utilitarian' a view of education.

It is a surprise to discover, therefore, that the British were
well aware of the link between education and economic
prosperity in the nineteenth century, indeed this was the
impulse behind the beginning of a state education system.
When the first education bill was introduced to the House of
Commons in 1870, the President of the Board of Education,
W. E. Forster, stated plainly that 'upon the speedy provision
of elementary education depends our industrial prosperity
. . . It is no good trying to give technical training to our
artisans without elementary education.' Fifteen years before
Mori Arinori created a state education system in Japan with
a technical bias, the British had grasped the critical relation-
ship between education, technology and prosperity. But

whereas the Japanese did something about it, the British did not.

The elementary education that Forster's bill provided was strongly influenced by the academic curriculum and ethos of the existing public and grammar schools. It was well over a hundred years before the Education Reform Bill of 1988 gave technology a secure place in the national curriculum. The blame for this failure – disaster would not be too strong a word – lies with the British ruling class and with their public school education. A nineteenth-century public-school education inculcated attitudes that seemed admirable at the time but that predisposed the pupils to be ignorant and contemptuous of manufacturing industry. Upper-class distaste for trade and industry was not unique to Britain. But it was only in Britain that this attitude took such a firm hold. No other country had a network of private boarding schools which virtually monopolized the education of the ruling class and taught them the superiority of a career in the professions and the public service. The nineteenth-century public school boy was neither as snobbish nor as unimaginative as his caricature suggests, but he left school convinced that no gentleman would become an engineer or an industrialist or a tradesman.

The consequences of prejudice were far-reaching. It delayed the introduction of science into the curriculum and delayed the introduction of technology even longer. It encouraged the British to underestimate the importance of industry. Above all, it reinforced the view that as education had no utilitarian goal, there was no necessity for the state to have any say in the curriculum.

This emphasis on academic rather than practical subjects, on pure science rather than applied, on qualities of character rather than useful skills, soon permeated the emerging state school sector. It is hardly surprising that the technical schools envisaged in the 1944 Education Act did not develop. The public school snobbery about technology infected the whole population. It will always be impossible to prove that the attitudes inculcated by the education system were a major – perhaps the major – reason for Britain's industrial decline. 'What is cause and effect in history?' was a familiar question in Oxford General Papers. In this case, however, the connection between cause and effect could hardly be clearer. If an anti-industrial bias in the education system coincides with a period when the country's industrial performance is overtaken by one competitor after another, it is perverse to argue that the two facts are not connected.

There may be disagreement on how education should be reformed so that the connection can be made beneficial rather than harmful, but we can no longer argue that as far as economic prosperity is concerned it does not matter what you teach or how education is organized. The lesson of the last hundred years is that it does matter so that one of the aims of British education must in future be to contribute to the country's economic prosperity.

The need to mobilize education in the cause of social cohesion is less widely accepted. Whereas few people would now deny that the school curriculum must take account of the economy's need for a well-educated and well-trained population, the concept of social cohesion touches sensitive issues particularly in relation to the treatment of ethnic minorities. The diversity of culture and language in inner-city schools – in some of which over a hundred different languages are spoken by the children – raises the question of social cohesion in its most acute form. How far should schools go to integrate the children of ethnic and national minorities? There are those who believe that integration is itself a racialist idea and that schools should positively encourage the diversity of culture and language. I hold the opposite view. If ethnic communities wish to keep alive their language and culture that is their responsibility. The responsibility of schools is to give children a command of the English language and an understanding of British culture and values. Without these the children of ethnic minorities will never make sense of or come to terms with the society in which they live.

The British are so new to the problems of cultural diversity that they are frightened of being accused of trying to impose their own culture on the children of ethnic minorities. When I discussed this with a group of teachers they argued that to teach Asian or Afro-Caribbean children British cultural values was – to use their phrase – 'a form of cultural imperialism' based on the assumption that our culture is superior. This reaction reflects the muddled logic of the teachers rather than the long-term interests of the children. Teaching a common cultural heritage to all children is not imposing a superior culture on them. If I give travellers a map of the country through which they will have to pass, I am not imposing a superior topography on them; I am providing them with the information they will need to find their way.

The need to provide children with a cultural map is recognized in countries as different ideologically as the USSR and the USA. In both countries, the problem of reconciling diversity and unity is made complex by the variety of national and ethnic traditions within their borders. Their approaches are different but the result is much the same. In the USSR, common cultural values are imposed on the education system by the central government. In the USA, the federal government has no direct influence on what is taught in schools but America's cultural heritage is taught to all children just the same.

I sat once at the back of a senior class in the Bronx High School of Science in New York. The pupils, reflecting the city's ethnic diversity, seemed to have come from every corner of the globe. They were studying Mark Twain's *Huckleberry Finn*. Whatever their origins, they were coming to terms with American culture and American values through the medium of American literature. Later the same day I took a history class in a high school in Manhatten. I asked them what they had been studying. 'The Revolution!' they cried. I should have known. Almost without exception, local school districts and individual schools throughout the United States make American history and American literature required courses.

Britain's population in the 1980s is not as culturally diverse as those of the USA and the USSR, but it is diverse enough to make the teaching of a common heritage essential both for the sake of the children and in the interests of social cohesion. This will not happen spontaneously because Britain, unlike the USA, has for so long been used to taking social cohesion for granted. It falls on the central government, therefore, to ensure that schools do not ignore this aspect of education.

In this chapter I have quoted explicit statements of the aims of education put forward in other countries and at other times. They range along a spectrum from the most liberal interpretation of what education is for to the uncompromising view that education is for the sake of the state. Changed economic and social circumstances make it impossible for Britain to continue to be vague about what it expects its schools to achieve. Britain, too, needs an explicit statement of educational aims. I think it should be along the following lines:

'The aims of British education are to develop the abilities of individual children so that they become independent-minded adults; to teach all children the skills and attitudes they will need to find employment and to contribute to national prosperity; and to ensure that all children understand the language, history and cultural values by which our society has been formed'.

That statement covers the three elements I have discussed: the liberal tradition of educating the individual (including the down-to-earth expectations of the parents), the economic demands of the state, and the requirements of social cohesion. The next step is to work out how these aims can be achieved.

3

WHAT SHOULD BE TAUGHT
IN SCHOOLS?
I

Who should decide?

Who should decide what is taught in schools? Until 1988 the British response to this question has been to argue that whether or not schools are free to decide their own curriculum is one of the touchstones of democracy. They have identified the teacher's freedom with the mainstream of British liberty. But a common school curriculum decided by central government is not inconsistent with democracy. It happens in democratic countries across the world from France to Japan. It also happens in undemocratic countries such as the Soviet Union. What distinguishes the undemocratic country is not central control of the curriculum but the use of the curriculum as an instrument of political propaganda. Those who argue that this could happen in Britain are expressing doubts not about the national curriculum but about the health of our democracy.

The confusion on this issue in Britain echoes a similar confusion over the introduction of compulsory military service in 1916. Military conscription, like central control of the curriculum, was identified with foreign despotism – 'Prussianism' and 'Tsarism' being two of the fashionable ogres – and was regarded as entirely alien to the traditional liberties of an Englishman. The truth was rather different. The British had managed to avoid military conscription not because they loved liberty more but because the channel made them virtually invulnerable to invasion. It was not a noble principle but a fact of geography that allowed the British to rely on voluntary recruiting for so long.

In much the same way, the British have avoided a national curriculum until now not through love of freedom but because they believed they were invulnerable to national decline. It did not matter what was taught in schools: Britain was doing very nicely with a decentralized, do-as-you-please education system. A national curriculum, like conscription, was a measure that foreign (by which the British meant 'inferior') countries found it necessary to impose.

When conscription was introduced in 1916 it was a pragmatic decision. For the first time, the British had to field a continental army on a scale that voluntary recruiting could not provide. When the national curriculum was introduced, British pragmatism was again responsible. There was no principle involved, no traditional liberty at stake. For the first time the British had to take education seriously. National decline had occurred and on a scale unimaginable a hundred years ago and the country was competing for markets with nations such as Japan whose school curriculum was geared to the needs of the economy. Britain could no longer afford to rely on a 'voluntary' education system.

If there is no preconceived principle involved, the question of who should decide what is taught in schools should be discussed solely in terms of pragmatic necessity. The safeguard against the abuse of central control is democracy itself. The necessity of central control of the curriculum is now widely accepted in Britain, and it is hard to imagine that any future government will abolish the national curriculum. But the policy still has its opponents. These include the people who remain sceptical of the need and those who continue to see central control as undemocratic.

I have some doubts about the motives of the latter group. Why do they persist in seeing a threat to democracy where no threat exists? Characteristic of their approach was the commentary on the Education Reform Bill published by the largest teachers' union, the National Union of Teachers, in January 1988. What the Union *says* it objects to is that the Bill empowers the Secretary of State to control education 'in a fundamentally totalitarian and undemocratic manner'. The section in the Bill on the national curriculum is condemned as 'fatally flawed', not least because it is couched in the language of 'conformism and authority'.

That teachers do not like to be told what to teach is understandable. Even Japanese teachers, long-accustomed to central control of the curriculum, object if they think they are being required to create workers useful to the economy. But the British teachers have enjoyed such an extraordinary degree of freedom compared with teachers in most other countries that their objection to the national curriculum probably has more to do with the loss of this privilege than with a genuine concern for freedom and democracy. Those who remain sceptical of the need for a national curriculum argue that it was already being taught. It is true there were many similarities between what was taught in school and what is now laid down in the national curriculum. But there is a world of difference between 'many similarities' and a situation where all schools teach the same specified subjects for the same proportion of the timetable using the same syllabus.

A few illustrations of this difference will have to stand for many. The national curriculum requires 10% of the timetable in the fourth and fifth years of secondary school to be devoted to a modern foreign language. But under the free-for-all, a large proportion of pupils in these years were studying no languages at all. Teachers took it upon themselves to decide that these pupils were 'no good at languages'. History, too, was more notable for its absence; in many schools it was absorbed into a portmanteau subject called integrated humanities. Under the national curriculum history has to be taught as a separate subject. Science is the most glaring case of dissimilarity. The majority of girls under the old dispensation were studying only one science, in most cases biology. The national curriculum will ensure that all pupils study three sciences.

The dissimilarities between what was taught and what the national curriculum requires were inevitable. Anyone who has run a school knows that the subjects that are taught, the time allotted to them, and the syllabuses that are followed, are not dictated by the needs of society or solely by the needs of the pupils. The subjects taught will partly reflect the availability of staff, the time allotted will often be the outcome of a power struggle between academic departments, and the syllabuses will in many cases be chosen to suit the interests and the experience of the teachers. I chose to teach the French Revolution because it was the topic I was most interested in. Whether new subjects are introduced depends largely on demand and facilities. The national curriculum makes technology a compulsory subject, but at Westminster there was neither demand nor facility, so technology did not appear on the timetable.

A national curriculum is the only way to ensure that these differences do not occur and that in the words of the government's consultative document 'all pupils regardless of sex, ethnic origin and geographical location, have access to broadly the same good and relevant curriculum'. Claims that they already had access to such a curriculum or that giving them access represents a totalitarian and undemocratic approach to education are without foundation.

Once a country has accepted the need for central government control of what is taught in schools – and that, despite some echoing dissent, is the position in Britain – it faces a number of questions on how that control will operate, the first of which is, 'Who in practice should make the decisions?'

Central government control means what it says. The central government may take advice, it may consult, it may farm out the task of drawing up programmes of study in individual subjects, but the final decision on what goes in and what stays out should remain with the central government itself. In countries where central control of the curriculum is well established, that means control by the minister and his permanent officials. In Japan, the Minister of Education, Science and Culture decides the Course of Study on the basis of recommendations from the Curriculum Council which is composed of 'teachers, researchers and other persons of learning and experience'.

In France, the bureaucratic control is tighter, the Minister making decisions on the advice of his own powerful inspectorate. The relative influence of politicians and civil servants is difficult to gauge but my impression is that in these two countries it is the civil servants who hold the real power. Under the French constitution, parliament's responsibility does not extend beyond determining 'the basic principles of education' so that the bureaucracy has full control over the detail.

A civil service will always tend to draw effective power into its own hands. Whatever the constitutional position, on a subject as complex as the details of a school curriculum, politicians would have to get up very early in the morning to ensure that every detail was exactly as they wished. What is needed, therefore, is a system that does not allow the decision-making process to disappear into the labyrinthine corridors of the bureaucracy. In theory at least that is the system that Britain has set up by the Education Reform Act.

The Act gives to Parliament the power of decision over both broad policy and detailed implementation. How far Parliament will have the time or inclination to concern itself with the latter remains to be seen. The government of the day will always be able to use its majority to secure approval of what its Secretary of State proposes, but the criticisms and the argument will be out in the open.

The Act also provides for the establishment of a National Curriculum Council to make recommendations, as in Japan. The members of the Council are appointed by the Secretary of State and he is not bound to act on their recommendations. But the Council is a statutory body and its recommendations will be made public; neither the civil servants nor the Secretary of State who has to justify his policy to the House of Commons will be able to adopt a cavalier attitude to the Council.

It is too early to be sure how the British system will work. What is clear is that the power to make decisions over the content of the school curriculum has been taken out of the hands of teachers and others directly involved in education. Even the National Curriculum Council is not dominated by so-called educationalists. The Act required the Secretary of State to 'include persons who have relevant knowledge or experience in education'. The National Union of Teachers argued that *only* such people should be included, but Kenneth Baker would never have agreed to that. One of the fundamental ideas behind the Conservative critique of the old regime was that power in the educational system should pass from the producers to the consumers, from the educationalists to the parents and the employers.

I am glad to see that the decisions on the curriculum are neither made by nor decisively influenced by teachers. There should be a clear distinction between society, which decides what it needs schools to teach, and the teachers who carry out the task. Teachers are citizens; they take an intelligent interest in what is going on. But they have no special expertise or experience to identify society's needs. On the contrary, they are in some respects outside the mainstream of society, spending most of their working lives with children. The idea that society could safely leave it to the teachers to decide what the country needed from its education system appears in retrospect to be extraordinary.

So the central government controls the curriculum in the interests of the consumers, that is of society as a whole. Can it be trusted not to exercise that control in its own party interests? It would be naive to imagine that in a democracy politicians will never try to nudge the curriculum in the direction of the philosophy they favour. In Japan, the conservative Liberal Democratic Party has influenced the teaching of values so that these reflect conservative rather than progressive or egalitarian values. But that is a far cry from the Soviet Union where the party congress dictates education policy and the Ministry of Education has no choice but to implement the decisions of the congress. It is a far cry too from the more extreme form of totalitarian democracy such as existed in China during the Cultural Revolution, when history and foreign languages disappeared from the curriculum as part of an attempt to eradicate Western influence.

I think the safeguards against political manipulation of the curriculum in Britain are sufficient. Though Parliament can be controlled by the party in power and the National Curriculum Council cannot force the Secretary of State's hand, the two bodies will nevertheless act as a public check on attempts to use the curriculum to promote a political ideology. When Condorcet drew up his scheme for French education at the beginning of the Revolution, he thought it wise to argue for a specific prohibition: 'No public body should have the authority or the influence to prevent the development of new truths, or the teaching of theories contrary to its own political views or its current interests.' The British, more confident of their democratic tradition, would regard such a safeguard as unnecessary. Nor does it follow that because some local education authorities have in recent years come very close to imposing political ideology on schools, central authority will try to do the same. One of the advantages of centralized control of the curriculum is that Parliament makes it much more difficult for a party to get away with political indoctrination.

Some people fear that central control will inhibit innovation. I would argue that would be no bad thing, because too much curriculum innovation in the last twenty years has been inspired by educational fashion. In education as in other fields what is new seems better. The trouble with education is that you can never be sure that your innovation is an improvement on the old way of doing things. In medicine, you know that the introduction of vaccination is an improvement. But in education you do not know, nor will you ever know, that teaching history as part of a subject called Integrated Humanities is better than teaching history as a separate subject. It must always be a matter of opinion.

It does not follow that curriculum innovation should be resisted, only that claims that a new subject or a new approach will be better than the old should be treated with scepticism. Central control will not prevent innovation but it will act as a useful brake on the more exaggerated claims of the innovators.

Teachers fear that central control will also act as a restriction on their freedom to use their professional judgement. They know that in some countries central control means that the government has to approve all the text books that are used in schools. In others, the detailed definition leaves little to the teachers' initiative; in Japan, even the warm-up exercises before each gymnastic class are prescribed. Keeping in step with instructions from the centre becomes a major preoccupation of teachers in France: the *Bulletin Officiel de l'Education Nationale*, which is the sole source of authority on curriculum teaching methods and textbooks, is essential reading.

All this makes disagreeable reading to anyone brought up under the British system of decentralized government where the word bureaucracy is almost always a term of abuse. But the logic of the national curriculum is that the central government has to lay down the detailed syllabus of every subject it has decided to include. There is no natural compromise or stopping-place between the decision to impose a national curriculum and the detailed prescription of what is to be taught in each subject. To insist that all children study mathematics without adding what mathematical topics they must study at what age would be pointless.

I am not persuaded by the teachers' argument that this removes or intolerably restricts their academic freedom. Academic freedom does not mean freedom to teach what you like regardless of the wishes of those who are paying your salary. In the universities, it is not a restriction of academic freedom if the government agrees to fund some research projects rather than others. The latter have to seek their funding elsewhere. Academic freedom is only infringed if the government explicitly bans some research from going ahead. As Condorcet insisted, 'No public body should have the authority or the influence to prevent the development of new truths . . .'.

As far as school teachers are concerned, the only way a government could infringe their academic freedom is by forcing them to teach a particular interpretation of knowledge that suits its own political ideology. In Nazi Germany all teachers, from the kindergartens to the universities, were compelled to join the National Socialist Teachers League which was responsible for 'the execution of the ideological and political co-ordination of all teachers in accordance with National Socialist doctrine'.

In the Soviet Union, all subjects are taught in a manner which is not only ideologically acceptable but also actively political in the sense of inculcating a communist world out-look. Even in the kindergarten, the children are taught to master such phrases as: 'Lenin created the Communist Party. The Party continues the work of Lenin. It leads our people to a bright and happy life.'

I recognize that by selecting these totalitarian regimes as examples of the denial of academic freedom, I am avoiding some of the more subtle questions of political bias and I will return to these later when I discuss the teaching of history. For now, we do not need to be too subtle. A detailed syllabus in any subject prescribed by the central government may restrict the school teacher's freedom of choice – of which period of history to teach for example – but it does not restrict his academic freedom unless it makes him an instrument of ideological indoctrination.

A more technical criticism of central control of the syllabus is that in some subjects it flies in the face of what we know about the different speeds at which children learn. The prob-lem is said to be most acute in mathematics. It is estimated that there can be a seven-year difference between the age at which a high-flyer and a slow-learner grasp the same mathe-matical concept. Common sense and our experience with our own children certainly suggests that there are subjects in which children learn at different speeds. How do we reconcile this with the idea of a national curriculum that not only dictates the syllabus but also the targets that children are expected to have reached by a certain age?

I think the answer is that it is possible if we de-emphasize the difference between children, or, if that sounds too much like the jargon I deplore, we would reduce the differences by playing them down.

The whole thrust of Western education from Rousseau to

twentieth-century educational philosophers, such as Dewey, has been to emphasize the needs of the individual child, who should not have knowledge thrust upon him but be allowed to discover knowledge for himself at his own pace. Meanwhile, the whole thrust of Far Eastern education, particularly in China and Japan, has been to play down individual differences; where they exist, they should be removed by hard work not by allowing children to proceed at their own pace. The slow bird, says a Chinese proverb, needs to start out early. The Western educationalist would say that the slow bird must not be pushed too hard in case he loses heart and considers himself to be a failure.

I am not suggesting that education in other countries is always better than our own or that the lessons of one culture can automatically be applied to another. But those who argue that the national curriculum with its specific attainment targets – as they are called – cannot be applied to a subject such as mathematics because of the differences in children's rates of learning, should at least consider how they do this successfully in China and Japan. My own view is that the attainment targets may be just what is needed to turn our emphasis on individual differences and defects into a more positive assumption that all children with hard work can reach the standards that are set for their age group.

I believe that the central government must prescribe the syllabus for each subject in detail, as well as the targets for each age group, if the national curriculum is to be effective. I do not believe it is necessary for it to prescribe the textbooks, and I am reluctant to deny the individual teacher this area of choice and to impose on the education system the Orwellian structure that would be necessary to screen all the textbooks that schools wish to use.

In Japan, the Minister of Education, Science and Culture has to authorize all textbooks used in elementary and secondary schools. The author or publisher submits his text to the Minister for approval. The Minister consults a body with the haunting title of Textbook Authorization and Research Council. On the basis of the Council's recommendations, the Minister draws up a list of authorized textbooks and sends the list to the local boards of education. The boards then decide which of the authorized textbooks to use in their schools. Private schools also must use books from the prescribed list.

The heart sinks at the imagination of such bureaucracy and soars again at the realization that not all is perfect in Japanese education. Japan's desire to censor school textbooks dates back to state direction of education in the last century and was not abandoned in 1945 because the Japanese government was unwilling to let teachers decide which version of the nation's role in the Second World War was taught to the children. In France and Russia control of textbooks also has historical roots. Allowing teachers to decide which textbooks to use is just not part of the tradition in either country. In France, the Church controlled the textbooks in the ancien regime; under the various revolutionary assemblies and under Napoleon, the control was if anything tighter. In Russia, too, censorship of textbooks was one of the elements of continuity between the Tsarist and Soviet regimes. Even though Gorbachev has eased the censorship of sensitive historical topics, what the textbooks contain is still controlled by the state.

In Britain, the government has stated that under the national curriculum the choice of textbooks is a matter for teachers. A future government may disagree. It is not difficult to imagine circumstances in which public opinion or parliament would demand that a particular book was banned. Under the Education Reform Act, the Secretary of State is not explicitly barred from extending his control to textbooks. Whether that extension is ever made will depend largely on the good sense of head teachers. If they do not exercise responsible oversight of the books that are used in their school, then the central government will be tempted to do so.

Before considering which subjects should be compulsory for all children, I want to return briefly to the question I raised in the last chapter, a question that will recur often in this book. I argued that the imposition of a national curriculum was not incompatible with an education that developed the individual's independence of mind. Am I still confident that is true in the light of the detailed instructions the central government is bound to issue in order to make the national curriculum effective? Even without prescribing textbooks, the government's grip on what is taught seems to leave little room for the encouragement of enquiring and independent minds.

I remain confident because I believe that the individualist tradition that has characterized Anglo-Saxon education is resilient enough to flourish within the framework of a national curriculum. But I recognize that this is a critical question. It is much more widely debated in the United States than in Britain. Americans ponder the economic power that has risen in the Far East, the immediate challenge of Japan, the more remote threat of China and ask themselves how far they will have to compromise their education tradition in order to meet the challenge of these new economic competitors. What worries them is that they see authoritarian education as the enemy of the open mind. Should they risk losing a degree of open-mindedness in order to match the Asians in their educational achievement?

Underlying all discussions about central control of the curriculum in Britain is this tension between the individualistic and the authoritarian approach to education. In the past, the example of France and Germany made us aware of this tension, but it has been the rise of Japan in particular that has forced us to face its implications. If we swing too far towards the authoritarian approach, will we stifle the independent-mindedness that is both the guarantee of our democracy and the mainspring of our best scholarship? Even if I am confident that we will never make that mistake, I need to keep the question in the forefront of my mind.

What subjects should be compulsory for all children?

Everyone has an opinion on what should be taught in schools. Designing a curriculum does not require special expertise (though educationalists naturally insist that it does). All you need is a clear idea of what the aims of your school system are and a stubborn inclination to ask 'why?' The curriculum is not a royal enclosure; no subject has a god-given right or hereditary title to inclusion. Either it has a specific usefulness or it is just an out-of-school pastime. But do not jump to the conclusion that this utilitarian test favours, say, chemistry rather than Latin. A good case could be made out for the usefulness of Latin as an instrument for teaching accurate communication. An equally good case could be made out that for most children the chemistry they learned in school has been of no use to them whatsoever.

Just as there is no such thing as education for its own sake, so there are no subjects that are worth studying in school as an end in themselves. That is not as philistine a statement as it sounds. Usefulness does not automatically mean usefulness in the market-place. Nor does it only imply obviously useful skills such as the ability to programme a computer. One of the most useful skills a boy learns at school may be his ability to evaluate evidence, a skill he acquired from the study of Anglo-Saxon history. But if a subject cannot be seen to have any utilitarian value whatsoever, it has no place on a school timetable.

In the nineteenth century, Cardinal Newman tried to distinguish between 'useful' education and education whose object was to produce intellectual excellence. I think that is a false distinction. What is this intellectual excellence? Newman defines it: 'To open the mind, to correct it, to refine it, to enable it to know, and to digest, master, rule and use its knowledge, to give it power over its faculties, application, flexibility, method, critical exactness, sagacity, resource, address, eloquent expression.'

These are admirable qualities but they are just as utilitarian as learning how to programme a computer. They are qualities that the possessor can turn to his advantage in any walk of life that requires clear thought and clear expression. I have quoted Newman out of context but I wanted to dispel the idea that some subjects are special and more noble because the particular skills and knowledge they impart could never be applied.

All subjects are useful. Some are more useful than others. That is the starting-point for designing a curriculum. The only way to judge a subject's usefulness is by reference to the aims of the education system. It is no good arguing that all children must learn a foreign language unless you are clear how that skill will contribute towards the achievement of your aims. What I am going to do, therefore, is to take each of my aims in turn and translate them, if possible, into subjects on the curriculum. Then I shall compare my curriculum with others and with the one that is prescribed under the Education Reform Act.

Let me remind you, then, what I think the aims of British education should be: 'The aims of British education are to develop the abilities of individual children so that they become independent-minded adults; to teach all children the skills and attitudes they will need to find employment and to contribute to national prosperity; and to ensure that all children understand the language, history and cultural values by which our society has been formed.'

The successful achievement of the first of these three aims depends more on *how* children are taught than on *what* they are taught, more on the expectation of the educators than on whether this or that subject is in the curriculum. I do not wish to anticipate a discussion that belongs in the next chapter, except to say that what is at issue here is whether a particular style of teaching is more likely to encourage independent thought; and whether the development of childrens' abilities can be accelerated and held back by the expectations of the teacher.

It is possible that some subjects give the teacher more opportunity to encourage independent thinking than others. Cardinal Newman would certainly have argued that this was the case. He would have prescribed a liberal arts education with particular emphasis on the study of the Greek classics, but I am not convinced that this is the only or even the best vehicle for helping pupils to develop independent minds.

As is so often the case in education, the evidence is largely subjective and anecdotal. When I try to identify the individuals I have known with truly independent minds, I think of two scientists who were both Nobel prizewinners and masters of Trinity College, Cambridge. The range of their intellectual interests and their ability to approach a topic without prejudice was in striking contrast to the often narrow and opinionated views expressed by some of the non-scientific dons at Trinity High Table. But the example of the Nobel prizewinners may be misleading. Maybe it was the independent minds they brought to science rather than the independent minds that science encouraged in them that made the difference. Yet scientific enquiry at its best is synonymous with curiosity, willingness to use and appraise evidence, flexibility, and an open mind.

The trouble is that our attitude to science as an instrument of humane learning and independent thought is coloured by our encounters with dull science teachers at school. High-quality scientists seldom go into school-teaching; high-quality history or English specialists often do. As a headmaster, I found that those who taught on the arts side could usually run rings round the science staff when it came to reasoned argument. Clearly the study of science does not automatically develop an open mind.

A similar uncertainty surrounds another piece of anecdotal evidence. One test of the independent-mindedness of a citizen is his refusal to conform to the dictates of a totalitarian regime. Can it be chance that so many of those who have been prepared to stand up against such regimes have been scientists? Is it because they have more independent minds or because they happen to have more courage or because the internationalism of science offers them some protection? I am not sure, but I note how few historians in Nazi Germany or the Soviet Union were unwilling to toe the party line.

As far as achieving my first aim is concerned, I have clear ideas about how we should teach and what expectations we should have of our pupils, but the curriculum remains a blank sheet. English teachers at Westminster used to tell me that boys should not be allowed to spend too much time on computers because it closed their minds. I remain sceptical of that argument and of Cardinal Newman's. The idea that some subjects close the mind and others open it is to me unproven.

My second aim – 'to teach our children the skills and attitudes they will need to find employment and to contribute to national prosperity' – is easier to translate into subjects on the curriculum. The danger, for Britain, is that having taken an aristocratic view of education for so long, a view that disqualified a subject if it was thought to be useful for trade or manufacture, we will now go overboard for those very same subjects in an attempt to compensate for our past omissions. And we may be tempted to translate national prosperity too literally, as though business studies on the curriculum would make our exports more competitive overnight.

The economic benefits of education are not that simple to obtain. Subjects such as science and technology must have a place on the curriculum but they do not of themselves constitute a philosopher's stone that will turn base metal into gold. As for business studies, it is a good example of the short-cut delusion. Though not as ludicrous as believing that peace studies will reduce the chances of world war, the idea that business studies in schools will improve our economic performance is based on a total misunderstanding of the way education can affect the economy.

We do not have to look at countries with successful economies such as West Germany and Japan to discover the secret of the relationship between education and economic prosperity. W. E. Forster explained it to the House of Commons in 1870. In a rural economy you only need to educate a few; prosperity is sustained by a large number of unskilled labourers. Even in the early days of industrialization, it was still possible to get away with a largely uneducated population because the number of skilled jobs in the factories and the mines was comparatively small. But once the balance in industry began to shift to more sophisticated technology, particularly to the high technology of the late twentieth century, a well-educated population became essential.

The secret of the relationship between education and economic prosperity in our own time is not children visiting factories or turning lathes or studying business: it is achieving a high level of education across society. This is the most striking feature of both the West German and Japanese education systems. The most striking feature of the British education system is the low level of education it provides for the majority of the population. In other words, British education is still geared to nineteenth-century economic conditions.

That still leaves us with the question of the curriculum. Does the high level of education have to be achieved in particular subjects? Now at last we can have a specific answer. Whatever else a well-educated population means in the late twentieth century, it means first and foremost that the citizens have been given a mastery of their own language – of the language of the country in which they live – and of mathematics.

A sense of anti-climax at this point would be understandable. Have we travelled so far in argument only to arrive at literacy and numeracy? No, that is not where we have arrived. Literacy and numeracy imply only an elementary grasp of these skills. What I am talking about is 'mastery'. British schools teach literacy and numeracy but too many pupils leave unable to write clear, accurate English, while all but the simplest mathematics remains beyond their reach. Even the most ardent supporters of British education now accept that children in West Germany and Japan are far ahead of their peer group in Britain when it comes to the mastery of mathematics. It would be for the central government to define what topics and concepts need to be mastered, but a simple rule of thumb would be that no pupil on leaving school should be disqualified from training for a *skilled* job because of the limitations in the standard of his or her English or mathematics.

It is not making English and mathematics compulsory for children throughout their schooling that matters – that is already the case – but the intervention of the central government to force schools to translate periods on the timetable into effective mastery of the subject. That is why it is so important that the central government (as the British government now intend to do) prescribe the syllabus, set the targets or level of mastery for each age group and test pupils' progress at regular intervals. This is the crucial difference between the old system and the new, between aristocratic and national education: the central government, not the educationalists, decide what our expectations of children should be and provide the mechanism to ensure that those expectations are fulfilled.

English and mathematics should dominate the curriculum in the primary stage of education. The other subjects that will form my version of the national curriculum will play only a small part in the primary school timetable. When I describe these subjects as compulsory, I mean that all children must study them but that it is only at the secondary stage that the subjects take their full quota of periods on the timetable.

Mastery of your own language and of mathematics is the key to that well-educated population on which prosperity in the modern world depends. The claims of science to equal status with these two subjects is less convincing. In the British national curriculum it does have equal status; it is one of the three core subjects, the other compulsory but less important subjects being known as 'foundation subjects'.

Our elevation of science to the status of core subject while technology and a modern foreign language remain only foundation subjects, reflects our feelings of guilt at having treated science in a cavalier fashion in the past. Although science used to appear on the timetables of all secondary schools, most secondary school children were studying only one science which, in the case of girls, as has been said, was almost always biology. One of the scandals of British education since the war has been the failure to give girls in state or private schools a scientific education.

Equal status for science with the study of your own language and of mathematics is not a characteristic of the national curriculum in those countries where you might most expect it. Whereas in Britain, science will share with English and mathematics, 'the majority of curriculum time at primary level', in the first six years of compulsory schooling in Japan,

Japanese language, which is difficult to master, has three times as many hours, and mathematics twice as many hours, as science. In the same years of schooling in the Soviet Union, the predominance of language and mathematics over science is more striking; and even when they reach the last years of compulsory schooling Soviet children spend as much time studying Russian literature and Russian history as they do studying science.

The distinction between English and mathematics on one hand and science on the other is the distinction between what is fundamental and what is important. It is virtually impossible to cope in modern society without being literate and numerate but one could manage well enough with little or no scientific knowledge. Or to put it another way, I cannot start to learn science unless I am literate and numerate, but I can start to learn English and mathematics even if I have never heard of science. I have no doubt that science should be a compulsory subject, but in terms of achieving my second aim I would place it on a par not with English and mathematics but with technology and a modern foreign language. The implication of this is that in the first three or four years of compulsory schooling science, technology and a foreign language will play little or no part in the curriculum. Making our children scientifically literate does not require a policy of overkill. As in the case of all the other important subjects, the break with the past is achieved by making sure that the schools teach science effectively to a centrally prescribed programme.

The connection between science and technology on one hand and economic prosperity on the other does not require emphasis. The case for including a modern foreign language should be just as obvious. A hundred years ago, Cambridge sneered at the study of modern foreign languages because they might be useful in international trade, which is the very reason why we must insist on our children learning them.

The aim of creating a well-educated population in which to build individual and national prosperity has not led to a revolution in the choice of subjects but to the necessity of ensuring that these five essential subjects are effectively taught to all children. The demands of my third aim of social cohesion will add a sixth subject to the list – history.

I am surprised that it is controversial to suggest that children should know and understand the historical events that have shaped the society in which they are growing up. It is true that social cohesion is a term that can be interpreted in different ways. It is also true that totalitarian regimes use history not to give children a map of the country through which they must pass but to impose upon them a political ideology. Of all subjects, history is the most easily abused by the unscrupulous. I also recognize that the choice of which historical events and which interpretation to teach cannot be totally dissociated from politics, however scrupulous the central government is to avoid indoctrination.

Yet none of these legitimate considerations is a sufficient reason for not teaching children the story of history as it has affected our society. They need to know how our parliamentary democracy has evolved, for example, if they are to make any sense of belonging to British society. When the extreme totalitarian Khmer Rouge seized power in Cambodia in 1975 they made it a crime to think about the past: 1975 was Year Zero. A democracy should take exactly the opposite view. It is a crime not to teach children about the past of this country, whatever their national or ethnic origins. They are now part of a particular historical drama; they cannot understand what is going on unless they are told what has happened so far.

English, mathematics, science, technology, a modern foreign language and history are the compulsory subjects in my curriculum. I am going to add physical education for the simple reason that I want my well-educated population to be fit and strong. The British national curriculum differs from mine in that geography, music, and art are also compulsory, and science is given a special status. The Japanese and Soviet curriculum also make music and art compulsory. And look back to the French Revolutionaries, the first in modern times to tackle this problem. The various curricula they proposed tended to be severely practical: mathematics for land measurement and commerce, the French language to create unity, the study of the Constitution and the Declaration of the Rights of Man to make good citizens of the Republic. Their curricula, like mine, were dictated by what they perceived to be the aims of education.

That is where we began. A curriculum is not a hit and miss affair from which with any luck useful attributes will emerge. It is a means to an end.

4

WHAT SHOULD BE
TAUGHT IN SCHOOLS?
II

I have based 'my' curriculum on seven compulsory subjects, but I have only just begun to answer the question 'what should we teach?' I want to look more closely at some of the compulsory subjects, particularly where definition of the content is likely to be controversial. Then I shall turn to the options or electives, those subjects that are desirable but not essential, and I shall end by discussing some of the enemies of a good curriculum and some of the problems that are not easy to resolve.

Defining the content of the syllabus or programme of study under the British national curriculum is the job of subject working groups appointed by the Secretary of State. Some of these working groups have completed their task; others have not yet been appointed. My comments are not an attempt to *define* a syllabus. I am just drawing attention to issues that I think should be borne in mind if the compulsory subjects are going to deliver the goods as far as my aims of education are concerned.

What should be taught in science and mathematics is uncontroversial. *How* science should be taught and mathematics should be tested may provoke argument, but not the content of the syllabus. I am assuming that it is no longer controversial to insist (as I would) that the facts of sex and health education, including AIDS, are dealt with effectively in Human Biology.

Technology is not by its nature controversial either. But it does raise the question of precisely why the British have included it in their national curriculum. When Kenneth Baker argues that the point of compulsory technology is that 'even those who are academically gifted will have to roll up their sleeves and learn some craft', his words have an old-fashioned ring. Learning a craft does not sound like an adequate response to the modern challenge presented by countries whose schools produce a high level of general education for everyone.

Technology has been defined as 'the rational application of science to the human condition'. As a subject on the curriculum its aim should be to develop the skills that are required in the process of designing and making. Pupils presented with a practical problem must formulate a solution, create the necessary design and make the artefact. It does not matter what the problem is – schools have worked in such diverse areas as rocketry and costume jewellery; what matters is the ability and confidence to solve practical problems which is not the same as learning a craft.

That technology should at last come in from the cold is hardly surprising. The failure of the British to recognize the importance of technical education, the low social status accorded to engineers, the emphasis in schools on academic achievement and analytical skills at the expense of inventiveness and practical skills – this depressing catalogue is too well known to require elaboration here. Our acute awareness of these past failings has made us transfer technology from the outer fringes of the curriculum to the centre. Like Tsar Peter the Great of Russia and Mori Arinori of Japan, we have seen the necessity of using the education system to compete technologically.

The historical precedents should make us pause. Russia and Japan were so far behind the West they knew exactly what technology they had to teach to achieve a great leap forward. The aims of their technical education were specific. Similarly, the École Polytechnique in Paris, one of the most admired centres of technical education, was founded in 1794 to meet a specific demand for military and civil engineers.

The British motivation is not so clear cut. Are we hoping that compulsory technology will give birth to more engineers or are we trying to correct the anti-industrial bias in our culture? Are we doing penance for past sins of omission, or does technology in the curriculum have specific aims? If it is more engineers we are after it would be better to found our own École Polytechnique to establish the prestige of technical studies in higher education. It is by no means clear that technology *in schools* automatically produces more engineers. Both West Germany and Japan produce more engineers and have more successful economies than we do, but whereas West Germany has a long-established tradition of technical education, the Japanese have changed tack since the days of Mori Arinori. They now believe that a high level of *general* education in schools followed by technical training provided by the employer is the right formula. Japan's supply of engineers and her economic prosperity owes little to technology in the school curriculum because the subject is hardly present. In Japanese schools, industrial studies for boys are set against homemaking for girls, and it is clear that neither has a high priority.

The British Engineering Council has recently issued a joint statement with the Society of Education Officers in which it is claimed that technology in the curriculum will 'make a significant contribution to the long-term competitiveness of industry and commerce'. Maybe it will but that is not a cause and effect we can take for granted. There is, however, a more important motive for moving technology to the centre of the curriculum. Other countries at other times have needed a great leap forward in technical knowledge and skills; Britain needs a no less dramatic change in the *status* it gives to technical education. For us, the usefulness of technology in the curriculum depends less on exactly what is taught than on the extent to which its presence persuades the education system to take technology seriously.

The British do not lack aptitude for solving technical problems, they just lack respect for those who spend their lives doing so. The cultural bias is in the *attitude* not the *aptitude* of our children. I recall numerous pupils who were fascinated by technical problems but who were forced to divert their gifts to semi-criminal activities, such as tapping the masters' telephones, because the school provided no outlet for their interest. Such pupils had all the inventiveness and ingenuity required to solve technical problems but would never have dreamt of a career in engineering. The cultural bias wasted their talents. Technology in the curriculum will not automatically correct the bias any more than it will automatically pro-duce more engineers. All depends on the status it is given. The signs are that the British are now prepared to recognize that technology is not just a subject for the less intelligent who cannot grapple with abstract concepts. A-level design and technology is increasingly accepted as a qualification for university entrance. The Royal Society of Arts scheme 'Education for Capability' and the government's Technical and Vocational Education Initiative in secondary schools have also helped to establish the subject's credibility. But in many ways the most remarkable change has occurred in the independent schools where the anti-industrial bias was nurtured and where, until recently, academic snobbery treated technology with open contempt. In the last ten years, independent schools have spent millions of pounds on new technology buildings. In 1987, the schools set up a Centre of Design and Technology in Oxford to exchange ideas and information and provide inservice training for their teachers. If the prestigious independent schools are a guide to a subject's acceptability, technology has arrived.

Information technology is an essential tool rather than a separate subject. Every child needs to learn how to use a computer. The computer in turn will facilitate his learning in various subjects and will soon change the way he manages his school work. It might also shake the dust off some teachers. With a word processor, a sixth former can easily produce a corrected version of a history essay. The teacher who has been in the habit of writing perfunctory comments on the first version will have to think twice about the changes he is suggesting. In due course, information technology may challenge the concept of school as a place to which pupils need to go to learn. But the dislocation of school is some way off. For the time being one of the aims of technology in the curriculum is simply to ensure that pupils master the computer skills they will need at work and increasingly in everyday life.

'Mastery' – the more I reflect on what should be taught in schools, the more I find myself returning to this word. The pointlessness of so many hours in the classroom, the disproportion between labour spent and knowledge gained, may lead us to the wrong conclusion that this or that subject is a waste of time whereas it is the teaching not the subject that is at fault.

The need to achieve a degree of mastery is especially true of another compulsory subject, the modern foreign language. The British are said to be bad at learning other people's languages, though not as bad perhaps as the North Americans and the Australasians. I do not believe that learning languages comes more easily to some nations than to others. Mastery of a foreign language is a matter of motivation, not ability. A member of the bottom French set would be speaking fluent

French soon enough if he fell in love with one of the dancers at the Moulin Rouge.

What lies behind Britain's half-hearted interest in learning foreign languages is that they cannot see the point in doing so. In the past, an Englishman abroad who could not make himself understood raised his voice. It was up to foreigners to learn English. That arrogance would have died with the Empire had not the economic and military power of the United States made English the *lingua franca* of the world community. Just when the British thought they would have to take the learning of other people's languages seriously, the need to do so was removed.

Or so it seemed. Membership of the European Economic Community and the demands of international trade have denied the British the chance to continue with their linguistic arrogance. The worker moving freely in the EEC and the manufacturer trying to sell his wares in Brazil or Indonesia, cannot rely on shouting louder at the natives. Neither the aim of individual employment nor of national prosperity can be achieved if we ignore the need to teach a foreign language. That need will become more acute in 1992 when national barriers to working, selling and producing in the community are removed.

But which foreign language? Do we obey the economic imperatives and teach Japanese instead of French? I think this is a wrong approach. The School of Oriental and African Studies, which teaches some of the world's most difficult languages to students and businessmen, has no doubt that it is a great advantage to have mastered a European language first. The compulsory foreign language in the curriculum must be a language that is comparatively easy and that is not remote – culturally or geographically. Whether it is French or German, Spanish or Italian does not matter much. What does matter is that the children of a trading nation should acquire the confidence that they *can* master a foreign language, that they can break free from the Anglo-Saxon myth that some children 'will never be any good at languages'.

It may be argued that we do not need to teach all children French in order to provide a handful of businessmen and diplomats with the means of learning more difficult and useful languages. Dutch and Swedish children can see the point of learning English; it is their link with international communications. But British children will still not see the point of learning French or Spanish or Italian however much you tell them about the EEC and balance of payments. This objection is rooted in past attitudes: the arrogance of Empire and the Little England attitudes of our post-imperial culture. I think it is essential for British children now to grow up with a sense of being European. That is their economic base and in the twenty-first century Europe will increasingly be their political and strategic base too. Mastery of a European language is one guarantee that they will 'think' European. But I accept that if three lessons a week for five years leads to nothing more than the ability to ask a Frenchman the time of day, then the study of a modern foreign language is a waste of time. I cannot recall who first proposed that 'if a thing is worth doing, it is worth doing badly', but that is certainly not true of learning a foreign language in school.

It should not be true of learning your own language either. The essential characteristic of a well-educated population is its mastery of its own language. How obvious that sounds yet how fierce is the argument about what should be taught under the heading of English. The argument is part of the struggle between the traditionalists and the progressives and its *casus belli* could be summed up in the word 'grammar'.

The argument is more about means than ends though it is difficult to disentangle the two. The protagonists agree that the aim is to ensure that children are able to master the art of communication in their own language, that is to say they can understand and make themselves understood. There agreement ends. The traditionalists argue that there is such a thing as correct English, and that communication, particularly written communication, depends on its use. The progressives argue that there is no such thing as correct English. The use of language should be judged by its appropriateness to the occasion. No dialect is inherently superior to another, nor is written English more important to teach than spoken English. It follows that the traditionalists will emphasize that there are rules of grammar that define correct English, whereas the progressives insist that rules of grammar are descriptive not prescriptive, they describe how language is used not what is correct or incorrect.

Once upon a time, King Grammar reigned supreme. No one denies that his rule could be oppressive. His henchmen were the dry-as-dust teachers who imposed on children those obscure rules of grammar and syntax that Sidney Smith called 'the nonsense of the grammarians'. By the 1960s, King Grammar was ripe for overthrowing. Grammar was a predictable victim of the Swinging Decade. It was associated with authority, tradition and elitism. Grammatical rules, like so many other rules at the time were regarded as intolerable restrictions on personal freedom; they killed youthful imagination before it had had time to develop. Remove the restrictions of grammar and the creative juices would flow, though to what end was never entirely clear.

Many teachers believed that a piece of creative writing however inaccurately expressed was by its very nature more authentic (a word much in vogue at the time) and therefore superior to a piece in which the free flow of the imagination had been restricted by the rules of grammar. It was as though the master carpenters had decided to abandon the teaching of essential skills to apprentices so that the latter could start work with imagination as their only guide.

I do not understand how anyone can believe that it is possible to master a skill – whether it is communication or carpentry – without learning the techniques on which it is based. Creative writing has long been part of the good English teacher's programme but not as a substitute for teaching children how to use language correctly. Nor am I convinced by the argument fashionable in the 1970s and still influential, that because young children learn to speak the language spontaneously and then learn what is correct speech later, so when it comes to writing they should be encouraged to write spontaneously at first ('starting from where they are' to use the jargon) and then learn later how to bring that free expression under control. Like many progressive arguments, this one sounds plausible. But it assumes that the teaching of grammar is necessarily pedantic and dull, that children dislike learning rules, whether of grammar or arithmetic and that the rules of correct English restrict rather than release the imagination. My experience would not support any of those assumptions.

By the 1980s, King Grammar's émigré court was attracting an increasing number of influential visitors. I am in favour of his restoration but – to pursue the metaphor one step further – as a constitutional not an absolute monarch. The rules of grammar have no divine authority. They exist to serve us. Children need to learn those rules and *only* those rules that enable them to write lucid, accurate prose. They need to know how to construct a sentence, how to spell correctly, and how to punctuate their work so that it makes sense to the reader. A good grounding in correct English is not just an essential tool in a world dominated by communication. It is a filter through which half-truths and misleading generalizations cannot pass. It will not guarantee independence of mind but it will increase the chances of developing that quality. It will not guarantee a job but it will greatly increase the options that are available.

Mastery of the English language is part of the individual's survival kit. To put it at its lowest, if he cannot complete an application form or understand a notice on the factory wall, he will be restricted to one of the diminishing number of unskilled jobs. A literacy and numeracy survey in one of our major cities in October 1987 found that of twelve hundred 16- to 18-year-olds, 86% could not complete a simple application form correctly and 62% could not understand a notice telling them what to do in case of fire.

The progressives argue that such people should not be regarded as illiterate; they are only 'functionally illiterate', that is to say they can read and write but unfortunately not well enough to carry out the simplest tasks in adult society. That distinction will be no consolation to those who have so little to show for eleven years of compulsory schooling or to society whose investment in education produces such modest results.

In this context, it will appear almost laughable to talk about the importance of British children reading the classics of English literature. But I am concerned with what schools should be *aiming* to achieve. The first aim of English in the curriculum is mastery of the language. The second aim is to use that skill to give access to literature. In practice, after the earliest years, the two aims are pursued side by side, just as they are in teaching a foreign language. My motive for wanting children to read the great works of English literature is that these classics are an essential part of that map of British culture that all children need. For this reason, I believe that central government should prescribe certain authors for particular age groups. I am not suggesting that these should be the only authors to be read and studied; I just want to ensure that at the appropriate point in their school career, all pupils are given access to Chaucer, Shakespeare, Dickens, and so on.

That certain works of literature should be prescribed by the central government is anathema to most teachers of English. More than any other teachers, teachers of English dislike being told what to do. They argue that there is no agreement on who the great authors are and that anyway, modern, more accessible works have more relevance to the lives of the pupils.

There is no greater nonsense purveyed by English teachers than the idea that because an author lived long ago, his or her work is no longer relevant. A literary classic is always relevant because of the quality of its writing and insight into the human predicament, and because it is a landmark in the evolution of the culture. To offer the pupils *The Secret Life of Adrian Mole* instead of *Oliver Twist* is to impoverish their education in a number of ways. Dickens is an author whose greatness has stood the test of time and of international opinion. His novels open a window on to the Victorian society from which our own society has evolved. You will learn more about British attitudes – to children, to crime, to poverty, to property – by reading *Oliver Twist* than by reading any modern novel. You will also learn more about human nature from a writer of genius than from a writer of talent, however popular.

If I want to create a society in which there is a sense of unity and social cohesion, I must ensure that the children share the common experience that English literature provides. That is not the same as saying that I want to influence their political attitudes through the medium of literature. In the Soviet Union literary texts are used as a medium for ideological education. What I am trying to achieve through the medium of literature is a sense of belonging to a particular society and an understanding of how that society evolved. My aim in prescribing *Oliver Twist* is not to prompt any 'right' moral or political response to the social conditions of Dickensian London, but to give children some insight into the society that is the great-grandfather of their own and to make them aware that British culture is a continuum of which they, as well as Oliver Twist and the Artful Dodger, are part. Whatever the virtues of *The Secret Life of Adrian Mole* and other so-called 'youth-orientated books', they cannot give pupils this insight and this awareness. They are not landmarks on the map of our culture.

I have no doubt that there are those who would like to see that map eradicated. At Stanford University in California a group of minority students and radical faculty members protested against a freshman's course in Western culture with the chant: 'Hey, hey, ho, ho, Western culture's got to go.' It is a sentiment that is reflected in the choice of English texts not only in some of our schools but also in some of our examination boards. A national curriculum ought to ensure that Western culture does not fall victim to those who by design or default suppress the classics of English literature.

History, like literature, is a medium through which children develop a sense of belonging to a particular society. The aim of history as a compulsory subject is not – as supporters of the new GCSE syllabus argue – to teach 'the skills that historians commonly use'. It is to help children to understand the society in which they live and through that understanding to find common ground with their compatriots. If in the process they learn how to evaluate evidence, to spot bias, to set out an argument clearly, or just to enjoy a good story, that is a bonus. It is not the principal aim of the exercise. All British children should study British history. Whatever other history courses are available – European history, American history, world history – they should never take precedence over British history. History, like charity, should begin at home. Nor should we fall into the same trap as the advocates of modern, youth-orientated literature. Modern history is not more relevant to our purpose than the history of the Civil War or the British Empire. Bad teachers, desperate for their pupils' attention, turn history into current affairs. I am reminded of school chaplains in the Sixties who were forever praying for peace in Vietnam as though only today's headlines could make the business of talking to God at all credible.

The yardstick by which to judge which events to include in the syllabus is their contribution to our understanding of the way our society – and that includes our national characteristics and attitudes – has evolved. Prescribing what historical events must be taught will provoke as great an outcry as prescribing works of literature that must be studied. The example of Nazi Germany will be trotted out again. What strenuous service that example does in the interests of muddled thinking! The fearful need to remember that we live in a democracy. A totalitarian state or a Tudor monarchy can distort the past to suit its political ideology or legitimize its seizure of power. But in a democracy such as our own, a party in office would make itself a laughing stock if it was caught with its hands in the history syllabus.

I understand the desire of men in power to rewrite history (as a headmaster I did it myself by playing down the achievements of previous regimes) but we need to keep the dangers in perspective. Even totalitarian regimes do not find it easy to harness the school system to its propaganda wagon. *In Hitler's Germany*, Bernt Engelmann's account of growing up under the Nazis, suggests how unsuccessful the regime was in winning the hearts and minds of school pupils by doctoring the curriculum.

Children can spot a preacher a mile away. If a history teacher is using his lessons to plug the party line, most pupils will switch off. Paradoxically, it is in the sixth form, not with younger pupils, that the ideologically motivated teacher can have some influence because sixth-formers are more vulnerable to the flattery of sophisticated argument. The ideologically motivated teacher is rare. The biased history teacher is – I am glad to say – commonplace. His bias is not only harmless; it may be an asset. If he regards Charles I as a saint and Oliver Cromwell as a sinner, if he is a passionate admirer of Napoleon, if he believes that Crusaders and Conquistadores were a civilizing influence, in short, if he draws the line between enthusiastic prejudice on one hand and political indoctrination on the other, his bias will corrupt no one and will give spice to his teaching.

So I have no serious misgivings about central government direction of the history syllabus. If we are clear that the aim is to tell the story of how our society and its institutions evolved the problem of what to put in and what to leave out is not difficult to resolve. Nor is the question of interpretation. What children need to learn are the facts: what happened during the civil war and how it altered the relative power of the monarchy and parliament. Complex discussions about whether a marxist or a non-marxist interpretation of the facts is correct have no place in a curriculum for 5- to 16-year-olds. The unfolding drama is what matters.

At one time I regarded the chronological approach, starting with Roman Britain and finishing in the twentieth century, as hopelessly unimaginative and sterile, but now I think it is the best way to tell the story. Instead of starting from 'where children are', that is where you end. For the younger children, I would add to the history syllabus, the myths and legends that – for want of a less pretentious phrase – are part of our national memory. King Arthur and Robin Hood are as much part of English culture as real historical figures, perhaps more so.

I can sum up my attitude to literature and history in the curriculum in the following way. Imagine you are a foreigner who knows little about Britain or the British. You are appointed to an important post, perhaps in your country's embassy in London. You have time to prepare yourself. It is essential to your job that you understand what makes the British tick, what their attitudes are and what sort of society they have built. What would you do? You would look for answers in an outline of British history and in some key works of English literature.

That is what I want literature and history to do for our children. They are strangers of a sort because they are young and inexperienced. Through history and literature they should know the society they are living in at least as well as a foreigner whose job requires him to do so.

Optional subjects

My seven compulsory subjects would not occupy the whole timetable. About one fifth of the teaching time in a secondary school – 7 periods in a 35-period week, 8 in one of 40 – should be available for options, those subjects that are not essential but that a good curriculum would make available. The principal options should be geography, music, art, a second modern language, Latin, Greek and domestic science. Each of these subjects will have its supporters who are convinced that it is an essential part of any child's education. But no subject can be said to be essential in a vacuum; it is only essential if the lack of it would make more difficult the achievement of the aims you have set for your education system. I do not believe that any of the options I have listed is essential to my aims but if my aims were different then of course some of the compulsory subjects would become options and vice versa.

We need not argue at length, therefore, whether technology is more important than music or history than Latin. It just depends on what you are trying to achieve.

I do not think school technology is a miracle cure for our

industrial ills but I do think that when all our children have to study it, the harmful anti-industrial bias in our culture will begin to change and that this will contribute to national prosperity. With the best will in the world I cannot see the use of making music compulsory for all children from five to sixteen. I am in favour of music and art being taught to all children in primary schools, because by doing so I am awakening an interest or a talent that children may *choose* to develop in secondary schools, but anyone who imagines that fifteen-year-olds can be compelled to appreciate or practise music or art is living in cloud cuckoo land.

History also helps me to achieve one of my aims (in this case social cohesion) but Latin, whatever its virtues, does not. The case of Latin is an interesting one. Together with Greek, it formed the core of the curriculum for hundreds of years. What is remarkable is not that these classical languages are now fast disappearing but that they hung on for so long. When I started teaching in 1955, the classics teachers still assumed that their subject was the highest form of education and that its place in the curriculum could never be challenged.

That complacency was one of the chief causes of Latin's decline. The teachers were too proud to defend their subject until it was too late. When they did try, they undermined the one clear argument for studying a complex and structured language. Mastery of Latin develops in the young mind a tenacity, an excellent memory and a discriminating use of words. It develops what might be called intellectual guts. Like one of those multi-exercise machines that stretch and strengthen every part of your physique, Latin makes the mind tough and flexible.

The Latin teachers made the mistake of trying to win back customers by making the subject easier. They turned it into a soft option in which the most rigorous task was to translate Latin into English. Instead of arguing the case for Latin in terms of the qualities of mind it developed, they fell back on secondary arguments; Latin was a help in learning modern Romance languages and it introduced children to the cradle of Western civilization. These were not convincing arguments. If a pupil wants to learn Spanish it is better that he should get on with it rather than have to learn Latin first. As for introducing children to the cradle of Western civilization it was always more of a dream than a reality. The vast majority of children who were made to study Latin never came within a million miles of 'the glory that was Greece and the grandeur that was Rome'.

Subjects such as music and Latin are options in my curriculum not because they have no value but because they are not essential. I would like to see many children study them in secondary school but I would not compel them to do so. Choosing worthwhile options to complement the essential subjects has become much more difficult in recent years. A host of new subjects has appeared. A few, such as computer studies, reflect the need to teach children a subject they did not have to learn in the past. But many others reflect nothing more substantial than educational fashion.

In the 1960s, many teachers lost confidence in the traditional subjects and went off in search of new subjects that they hoped the pupils would find more palatable. The justification for these new subjects was said to be their 'relevance', a concept that, with a little ingenuity, can be adapted to support almost any subject under the sun. But the real motivation for introducing new subjects was to recapture the interest of a generation of school pupils who had become rebellious and disaffected. An extraordinary degree of self-deception occurred in the education world whereby teachers first judged the value of a subject by the extent to which it might appeal to the pupils and only then constructed a rationale which claimed that the subject was essential to their education.

A good example of this process was the introduction of university subjects to the school curriculum. Instead of concentrating on giving children a good grounding in essential subjects, schools offered law, politics, sociology, philosophy and other subjects that had previously been thought to belong in the university domain. The advantage from the teachers' point of view was not just that these subjects had an aura of relevance and novelty; they were associated with the adult world. But they had no place in the school curriculum. Some required an intellectual maturity that pupils below the age of sixteen seldom possess; others elbowed out essential subjects, substituting a spurious relevance for the acquisition of important knowledge, politics and sociology, for example, elbowing out history.

The search for novelty and relevance produce some even odder subjects such as peace studies. The appearance of peace studies persuaded some critics that the KGB had taken control of our education system. But the subject is more laughable than subversive. The idea that by teaching peace studies to children you can reduce the chances of war or even persuade children to grasp the issues is so naive as to be almost charming. It has the flavour of those pacifist gestures of the 1930s: an Anglican clergyman thinking that if enough people would take a pledge not to fight, war could be averted or, George Lansbury, the Labour leader, finishing his speeches with the cry, 'Hurrah for Peace and Goodwill!' Teaching peace studies to children is on a par with these vain gestures. It should be banned not because it is harmful but because it is a waste of time. The fashion for peace studies – a fashion now fading – is a good example of a recurring phenomenon: the teacher with delusions of grandeur. Teaching is not a glamorous occupation; the teacher's role is important but necessarily mundane. Yet most teachers are well educated and have a lively, often idealistic interest in world affairs. So there can be a frustrating discontinuity between the ideal and the mundane. Faced with the routine of French verbs or elementary physics, the teacher may be tempted to think that what he should be doing is to teach the virtue of international understanding or the wickedness of nuclear war. He is no longer the unglamorous instructor but part of a grand design to make the world a better place.

There ought to be a touch of idealism in every teacher but it should never distract him from the main task. His job is to teach children, not to promote peace or international understanding. Whatever their personal ideals, teachers must educate for the world as it is, not for the world they would like it to be.

The good curriculum has more subtle enemies than naive idealists. One is the fashionable campaign to 'break the tyranny of school subjects'. Those who support the campaign do not want 'a subject-based curriculum' at all. They want a curriculum based either on subject areas, such as integrated humanities, or on skills, such as literacy and verbal skills. This is not just a question of changing the name on the timetable. The advocates of a curriculum based on skills in particular want to shift the emphasis of teaching away from knowledge to the acquisition of skills. The priority in learning science will not be scientific knowledge but scientific skills such as observing and measuring. This shift of emphasis is then expressed on the timetable as 'Maths and Science studies'. The acquisition of linguistic skills becomes 'Communication studies' and so on.

There is a character familiar to all headteachers, who sits in a corner of the staff room, and when you have outlined your revolutionary changes, asks in a quiet voice, 'Isn't that what we have been doing all along only under a different name?' How maddening I found him. How right he often was. So much educational innovation is not innovation at all. However you label the time, much of the traditional subject-matter, particularly in English and mathematics, is still going to be taught; good science teachers will still insist that their pupils learn both a body of scientific knowledge and scientific skills; and in good schools, teachers of different subjects will find opportunities to 'break the tyranny of school subjects' without the need for a pseudo-revolution in the curriculum.

Regrouping and relabelling subjects is a red herring masquerading as reform. Another enemy of the good curriculum – multicultural education – is more well-intentioned than its critics allow and more damaging to children of ethnic minorities than even the critics realize.

Discussion of this topic is bedevilled by confusion and hypocrisy, but most of all by our failure to define what we mean by a multicultural society. If we mean a society in which a number of different cultures are of equal importance, then Britain is *not* a multicultural society. There is only one culture – one language, one history, one religion – that constitutes and helps us to understand the mainstream of British life. Minority cultures are not inferior in quality but they cannot have the same status in education because they offer no insight into the way our society has evolved.

The responsibility of the education system is to steep children in mainstream culture. Those who advocate multi-cultural education will recoil from this idea. They want the curriculum as a whole to be adjusted to the needs of a multi-cultural society. I do not suggest that no adjustments have to be made. A school can be seen to value minority cultures by ensuring that teachers are sensitive to different cultural viewpoints, by making assemblies sensitive to different religious faiths, and by treating cultural diversity as an enrichment not an impoverishment of society. But the adjustments should not mean changes in the curriculum.

The multiculturalists have made a wrong assessment of the

children's needs. It is not in the interests of the children of ethnic minorities to perpetuate their 'separateness'. If they are going to live in British society, they need to be able to move within that society with confidence and a sense of belonging. They will never do that until they come to terms with the mainstream culture. In this sense, the sooner the children become British the better. It is the school's job to help them do so. It is the family's responsibility to keep alive the minority culture if that is what they wish. As the Jews in this country have demonstrated, it is possible to become British, to absorb the mainstream culture, without losing your own culture or religion.

The gap between the multiculturalists' approach and mine can be illustrated by the question of mother-tongue teaching. I want all children to master English. If that is not their first language, the schools must provide teaching of English as a second language. But the school should not teach ethnic minority languages.

The multiculturalists want the school not only to teach these languages but to give them the same status as English and other modern European languages, so that Bengali would be on a par with French or Punjabi with German. But the more schools encourage the children of ethnic minorities to speak their own languages the longer it will take for the children to regard English as the language of opportunity, the language that will help them pass their exams and get a job.

The multiculturalists and I at least agree on one point. Education cannot ignore the fact that British society now embraces more cultures and religious faiths than ever before. But whereas they want education to adapt itself so that it reflects the new pluralism, I want education to help the children of minorities to adapt themselves to the one mainstream culture. I do not underestimate the difficulty of putting either policy into practice but I think that mine will give the children a better chance of developing a sense of belonging to British society without jettisoning altogether their cultural heritage.

Two problems remain. Or rather many problems remain because arguments about what we should teach cannot be corralled in two chapters. But there are two that I cannot avoid if this attempt to define a good curriculum is to be anywhere near complete. The first concerns the education of girls and the second, the place of religion. One further problem – the teaching of values – I want to deal with in a later chapter.

The eighteenth-century Enlightenment did not extend as far as equal educational opportunities for girls. To the French revolutionaries who first tried to devise a national education system, the role of women was to perpetuate the race, to watch over the development of the new generation. Even Condorcet, who advocated the same education for girls as for boys, did so on the grounds that well-educated women would be in a better position to educate their own children. Napoleon would not even go that far. Girls should be taught their domestic duties. Academic competition was to be avoided: 'We do not want to excite their passions or to give play to the vanity which is one of the liveliest instincts of their sex.'

Despite all the changes in the role and status of women, something of that attitude to girls' education remains. In some girls' independent schools, the pupils are taught 'hostess skills' rather than technology. In state schools, they run the hospitality suite, preparing the food and serving it to visitors. In Japan, 'homemaking' is a required subject for girls only. Even in the Soviet Union, where the constitution guarantees the equality of the sexes, pupils in vocational schools divide for what are called 'labour training lessons', the boys doing metalwork while the girls do sewing.

It seems that we can never entirely escape the idea that education is preparing boys to be breadwinners and girls to be homemakers. Part of me wants to make that escape possible. One of the most important and least noticed consequences of the British national curriculum is that it will for the first time guarantee that girls have the same education as boys. Never again in a state school will it be possible to timetable technology against domestic science or to deny girls access to all three sciences.

I welcome this long overdue reform but cannot dismiss a nagging question. Whatever the changes in the role and status of women, the majority of girls are going to be mothers and homemakers for a part of their adult life. Do we leave it to chance that they learn the knowledge and skills required or do the schools have to take on a responsibility that at one time most mothers of daughters assumed to be theirs?

One answer would be to insist that both girls and boys had to pass a course on parenthood and homemaking. I like the idea but do not think it is realistic. I come reluctantly to the conclusion that in this one respect girls' education has to be different from boys' and that in prescribing a course in homemaking for girls only, the Japanese are probably right.

My view of the role of religion in education is more clearcut but I recognize that it would be difficult to enforce in this country. I am opposed to the teaching of religion in state schools. I am in favour of teaching about the importance of the Christian religion in the evolution of our society and our institutions under the heading of history. But religious instruction, religious education, divinity – call it what you will – should not be a separate subject on the timetable.

My reason for taking this position has nothing to do with the diversity of faiths in our society. I want to exclude the teaching of religion from schools because I believe that introducing children to religious faith is entirely a matter for the family. The state has no business operating in this area through the medium of education. Nor should the state, whose interest is in unity, reinforce religious divisions by funding denominational schools.

A proposal to keep religion and education separate would cause an outcry even though this separation is a key element in the constitution of some other countries, notably the United States. The British are not a religious people which is probably why they cling to the idea of religious education; it saves them the trouble of bothering with the subject at home. They also believe that a dose of religion at the start of the school day, like a cold bath, will help to keep the more disagreeable aspects of adolescence in check. I doubt whether it matters to them what branch of Christianity or what religion is on offer as long as it does the trick. Like Gibbon's Roman magistrates, they find all religions in this respect 'equally useful'.

This approach to religious education is cynical but practical. If you must have religion in schools, British hypocrisy is preferable to missionary enthusiasm. Even so I do not think that is enough to justify religion in the curriculum. If teachers cannot communicate simple moral values such as honesty or unselfishness without the aid of religion they are hardly fit to be doing the job.

There is, however, a minority in Britain whose approach to religion in education is neither hypocritical nor missionary. Whether they are Roman Catholics or Muslims they cannot separate education and faith; a secular education is for them a contradiction in terms. I respect their point of view but do not believe that it should be subsidized by the taxpayer. If religious groups want to run explicitly religious schools they should be free to do so but at their own expense. What is provided by the state should be completely secular.

What should we teach? First decide the aims of your education system, then decide what subjects you need to teach. Both these decisions should be made by the central government. No subject should be compulsory unless it is contributing to the achievement of your aims. In this sense, a good curriculum is strictly utilitarian. No subject should be allowed as an option unless it can be seen to complement the main thrust of the curriculum. That is the only test of a subject's relevance. There is no virtue in novelty for its own sake; nor is there any case for introducing vain gestures however idealistic. Despite the siren voices of 'communication studies' and 'scientific skills' the curriculum should still be based on single subjects. It should not be adapted to meet the needs of minority cultures but used to assimilate the children of those cultures into British society.

It would not worry me if such a curriculum was described as reactionary or traditional or old-fashioned, because the only yardstick by which to judge a curriculum is whether it is likely to achieve what you want it to achieve. Your *aims* may be described as reactionary but your curriculum cannot be. It is a machine. It either works or it does not. I think mine would work but like any curriculum its effectiveness would depend on how well the subjects were taught.

5

HOW SHOULD WE TEACH?

Education has this in common with religion: because it is difficult to prove that you are right, it is tempting to dispense with argument and to assert that you *must* be right and that those who disagree with you are heretics. This is especially true of the conflict of opinion on teaching methods. Educational bigots are not as dangerous as religious or racial bigots but they exist. No one has been burnt at the stake for advocating competition or for failing to believe in mixed-ability teaching but intolerance and missionary zeal are common features of the educational scene. Academic qualifications are no guarantee that the holder will think and act in a rational way. On the contrary, there is no one more intolerant than an intelligent man who has got hold of the wrong end of the stick. Such men will be familiar to anyone who knows – to draw a rather sinister parallel – the European witch craze of the sixteenth and seventeenth centuries. Educational bigots are not in that class but they do have some things in common with the witch-hunters. The latter, for example, justified their actions with learned treatises and with research that turned out to be bunk.

To suggest that all educational research is bunk would be to fall into the same trap as the bigots but some of it does fly in the face of common sense, and rather more of it goes to great lengths to prove the obvious. Her Majesty's Inspectors recently reported that 'research studies here and abroad have shown that the regular setting and marking of homework are associated with good education and effective schools'. Any parent could have told them that for nothing.

The combination of bigotry, fashion and questionable research has made it increasingly hard for parents to sympathize with the way their children are taught. What they believe to be the right approach – based on common sense, instinct and their own experience of bringing up children – is at odds with the methods adopted by the teachers. Nor are they reassured by teachers' explanations.

A friend of mine was surprised to find that his ten-year-old daughter had no textbooks in school. At the next parents' evening he asked why and was told that textbooks were 'restrictive'. He suggested that a textbook at least gives a child a security, a point of reference, a sense of knowing what the subject is about, but he was told that his view was old-fashioned. 'Research studies have shown', the teacher added, 'that children develop a better understanding of the material if they are not confined to textbooks.'

Most parents do not have the time or the stamina to pursue the matter but common sense tells them that it is they who have their feet on the ground and the teachers who have been carried away by fashion and dubious research. The same sort of exchange could have occurred over mixed-ability teaching, homework, competition, classroom discipline and all the other issues raised by the question 'How should we teach?' The gap between society's expectations and educational theory remains wide despite the counter-attack against progressive education initiated by the first Black Paper twenty years ago. The heyday of progressive zeal may have passed, but the influence of progressive orthodoxy is still strong.

Is progressive teaching or, to use one of its more baroque alternative titles, learner-centred pedagogy, merely a passing

fashion or is it an irreversible stage in the evolution of education? One way of answering is to look at learner-centred pedagogy in a worldwide context. Few developed countries were
not affected by the passion for progressive education in the
1960s. One that was *not* was the Soviet Union, which had got
this stage out of its system long before. Immediately after the
1917 Revolution, the Bolsheviks abolished exams, outlawed
homework and corporal punishment, replaced formal classes
with freely formed groups or circles, and encouraged pupils to
take part in running the school. This phase was later described
as 'experimental' and 'romantic'. Forty years later, the Soviets
must have smiled to see the West taking the romantic path.

China was just as abrupt in its adoption and rejection of
progressive education between 1965 and 1975. When the Cultural Revolution began its attack on the remaining aspects of
imperial society, Chinese education felt the full blast of the
Red Guards' egalitarian zeal. Examinations, rote learning,
didactic teaching, the pursuit of intellectual excellence, selection procedures and the authority of teachers were all swept
away. They were replaced by progressive education which
reflected revolutionary ideology. The schools received new
revolutionary names. The Garden Village Middle School in
Beijing was renamed 'Mao Tse-tung's Doctrine, Anti-Imperi-
alist, Anti-Revision Middle School of the Capital'. Ten years
later the Cultural Revolution had run its course. Plans were
announced to make China a world economic force by the year
2000. With new priorities, the nation rejected progressive
education. The Minister of Education, Zhov Rongxin, condemned child-centred education for denying the children of
workers access to intellectual knowledge and good learning.
Back came examinations, selection, emphasis on standards,
merit awards for good teachers, above all hard work. School
texts used during the Cultural Revolution were condemned
as too easy. Students of history had to learn facts again and

political lessons were replaced by academic subjects. 'Key' schools for gifted children were re-established. Deng Xiaping told a national education conference in 1978 that China was twenty years behind advanced countries in science and technology and he urged teachers to have a practical, down-to-earth approach to their task.

This cycle of revolutionary enthusiasm for progressive ideas in education, followed by a fairly swift reaction when it is realized that traditional methods are needed if the education system is to underpin economic development, suggests that child-centred teaching with its egalitarian spin-offs is not an irreversible stage but is indeed an experimental and romantic episode. The fact that it has not been rejected in Britain is partly because there is no all-powerful central government that can impose such an abrupt reversal of education practice and partly because Britain is still reluctant to connect education to economic prosperity. So the question of how *we* should teach is still concerned with the conflict between traditional and progressive methods.

As was the case in Soviet Russia and Communist China, the educational arguments are interwoven with arguments about social and political issues. In the 1960s and early 1970s, Britain was not in a state of revolution, but its priorities were social rather than economic. Progressive education came in on a tide of popular feeling in favour of social justice, a vague but appealing concept. By ending streaming based on ability or discouraging competition, teachers would be helping to build a fairer and more compassionate society. Social justice is not an ignoble goal (always assuming you can define what it is), nor do I think that it is wrong to use the education system to promote social ends – after all, social cohesion is one of my aims. Where the advocates of progressive education did and still do go wrong was in their belief that *teaching methods* should be judged on their social rather than their educational value. Competition in schools was bad because it encouraged children to be personally ambitious which in turn helped to create an every-man-to-himself society.

The only criterion for judging a teaching method is whether or not it enables children to learn. Competition is good if it does and bad if it does not. Whether it makes children self-centred and society more cut-throat is irrelevant. But if you try to judge progressive methods by this simple criterion of whether they work, you run into the statistical flak of education's religious war. Educational research supports the case for both traditional and progressive methods and so for the purpose of making a judgement is virtually worthless. It seems to me that the only way to judge teaching methods is in the light of common sense and experience.

The case for child-centred learning, which is the educational as distinct from the social or political springboard for progressive teaching methods, is based not only on Rousseau but also on the developmental psychology of Piaget. Children will learn better, it is argued, if education starts by taking into account their individuality, their interests and wishes, their different stages of intellectual growth and their different speeds of learning. What this means in practice can be defined in terms of its opposite, so-called didactic pedagogy, or in simple English, teaching that has the character of instruction. A caricature of the didactic approach would be a corporal instructing recruits on how to use a bren-gun. He has something to teach and they have something to learn. He tells them what has to be done and demonstrates how. They listen and observe and then try it themselves until they get it right. If a recruit gets it wrong he is told to try harder. The corporal knows nothing about learner-centred pedagogy. He is not concerned with the interests or the individuality of the recruits. He has a job to do and the measure of his effectiveness is how well and how quickly the recruits learn.

Why cannot school teaching be like that? It can. The didactic method was used for centuries and is still used in some countries and by some teachers in this country. But its opponents say that it does not work, particularly with young children in primary schools. They argue that the mechanical learning of tables or of verb declensions so that the child can in time do it without thinking, like the recruit who has mastered the bren-gun, does not enable the child to learn. He can perform the drill but he does not understand what is going on or why. With child-centred learning, though the child may appear not to learn so much, he will in fact understand more and that understanding will provide a more secure base for moving on to the next stage of his learning.

It is at this point that people not involved in education will be inclined to ask whether the conflict between didactic and child-centred teaching is really necessary. Surely effective teaching uses both methods. There is a time for didactic teaching and there is a time for children to discover for themselves, a time for being taught and a time for learning. The good teacher is the one who knows which method is appropriate for which subject, for which occasion and for which group of children.

Many teachers would share this reluctance to polarize teaching methods between the traditional and the progressive approach. They would like to be pragmatic not ideological in their choice of method but they are not always free to be so. Progressive methods have become the accepted orthodoxy in many state schools, just as traditional methods are imposed on teachers in some independent schools. So it is not possible to resolve the conflict simply by saying that good teachers will always choose the right approach. There are still issues of policy that have to be argued out. Of these the most important are competition, streaming, homework and exams.

Many state schools ban competition between children – for

marks, for a higher place in the form order, for a prize at the end of the year. Child-centred education demands that the child proceed at his own pace and achieve success on his own terms not in competition with his peers. No one whose child has been disheartened or turned off school altogether by his failure to keep up will dismiss the critique of competition lightly. It *can* have a depressing effect on the uncompetitive child or the child experiencing difficulty in a particular subject. Our twin sons who, because of dyslexia, found English difficult, were, at the age of nine, placed at the bottom of the form and the back of the class, simultaneously discouraged and devalued. Both are now at university, but it took them several years to fight back against that early discouragement. The mistake was the teacher's, but the competitive spirit of the school endorsed it.

On the other hand, competition can motivate children who would otherwise drift, it can encourage those whose efforts are seen to be rewarded, it can stimulate those who thrive on competition, and it can provide school and parents with a guide to how individual pupils are getting on. It is a mistake to be obsessed with competition, either to the extent of banning it or to the extent of allowing it to dictate the ethos of your school. There are independent schools, particularly for younger children, where the pursuit of marks becomes an end in itself. They are joyless places in which an 8-year-old can tell his parents in all seriousness that he has 'passed his peak' because he has fallen a few places in the weekly order. But it need not be like that. The leading boys' independent schools are more academically competitive than they have ever been but the possible harm done by competition is much less than, say, in Japan, because at a school such as Eton there are so many other ways a pupil can make his mark.

Competition clearly helps to motivate some children, perhaps most. How do we prevent it doing damage to the others?

One answer is by not overdoing it. The other and more important answer is that the school must be seen to value all its
pupils, not just those who compete successfully. The mark of
a good school is that it is not afraid of introducing competition. In a bad school where children do not feel valued for
themselves, competition will only make matters worse. The
one thing schools should not do is to be two-faced about competition. I visited a comprehensive school in mid-Wales
where the staff awarded marks but never published orders.
The head acknowledged that the pupils soon worked out for
themselves where they had come in each subject. 'But', he
added, 'we shall not have been seen to have endorsed it.'

Streaming versus mixed-ability teaching raises similar
issues. Pupils in the bottom sets of their year are said to live
down to the school's low expectation of them. I agree that this
will happen if the school does not take steps to prevent it. But
I doubt whether pupils are encouraged or deceived by being
placed in a mixed-ability group. In practical terms, it requires
a teacher of rare gifts to do justice to the range of ability in
such a group. In a streamed set the teacher at least has a job
more suited to his ability and the pupils are working and competing (for compete they will, whether the school likes it or
not) with others of a comparable standard.

Children should be streamed in mathematics and modern
languages because in these subjects the range of ability and
different speeds with which children learn make a nonsense
of mixed-ability teaching. The risk of damage to the motivation of those in the bottom set can be lessened by the school's
attitude. If the best teachers are always timetabled to teach the
top sets, the members of the bottom set will draw their own
conclusion. If the bottom set always finds itself in the grottiest
classroom, the feeling of being fobbed off will be confirmed.

I would also stream the forms in an age group so that in
form-subjects such as science and English the range of ability

is not too wide. And I would give the forms accurate titles. Attempts to disguise the stream by calling the forms '4 Red, 4 Yellow, 4 Green' and so on, fool no one.

Mixed-ability teaching is less widespread than in the 1970s because teachers have recognized the difficulty of making it work. Ideologically, however, many teachers are still committed to it. Their commitment is a good example of the way educational arguments become confused with social, political, even emotional ones. Some of these teachers want an Alice in Wonderland world where everyone is in the top set and no one is disappointed. For other teachers, streaming (like selection) represents what they dislike about the way the world is. They cannot change the inequalities of human life but in the little world of the school they can impose a rough and ready equality. Children are made to act out social and political ideals that are impracticable in adult society.

Laziness rather than frustrated idealism lies behind the hostility to homework. There are teachers who oppose homework because they associate it with the 'prep' set in independent schools. Others argue that homework reinforces disadvantages because cramped and overcrowded homes do not give all children a fair chance to do it. Even where homework is official policy, its setting and marking can be, to say the least, erratic.

There is no secret why some teachers dislike setting homework: it means more work for them. However conscientious and professional you may wish to be, there are times when you deliberately forget to set homework or you set work that does not have to be marked. Marking pupils' work is the bane of a teacher's life. I found it so and I have no doubt all other teachers do too. I am not at all surprised that more and more ways are found of reducing the amount of written work, either by condemning homework as elitist or by other steps such as emphasizing the importance of oral work in English.

Just setting homework is of little use in itself. But no research is needed to convince us that homework thoughtfully set and promptly marked helps pupils to master subjects, particularly by acquiring the discipline of working on their own. Opposing it on ideological grounds is just wrongheaded. It is the children from disadvantaged homes who have most to gain by acquiring that discipline.

It is hardly surprising that the countries or schools that appear to be most committed to the educational success of their children are the ones that give most emphasis to homework. Even at the primary stage, Japanese children may be doing two hours' homework a night. In the Soviet Union, the Ministry of Enlightenment had recently to caution teachers because some pupils in the higher grades were spending as much as five or six hours a night on homework. In the United States, pupils in the elite private schools have to spend at least twice as long on homework as their contemporaries in the public high schools, and the same contrast between independent and state-school demands on their pupils exists in this country.

Examinations have been attacked from a number of different standpoints. When the Cultural Revolution hit the Chinese education system examinations were the first casualty. Entrance examinations for schools and colleges were condemned because they favoured the children of the bourgeoisie over the children of workers and peasants.

The same criticism of exams is made in Britain by those who see public exams as the class system in operation. Because the middle class use exams as a way of restricting entry to their ranks, they design the exams so that it is middle-class children who pass. In the jargon, 'exams reinforce classism'. Less politically minded progressives criticize exams from a different standpoint. Exams encourage didactic teaching and run counter to the need to treat children as individuals, allowed to develop at their own pace. A more broadly based critique of exams emphasizes that they only test ability to pass exams, in particular the ability to memorize material and reproduce it on paper. They do not assess the pupil's understanding or his ability to think.

The various criticisms have led to some modification of the style of exams in the direction of more project work and more continuous assessment rather than a 'one-off' test at the end of the course. But the principle of public exams remains central to British education and was reinforced by the Education Reform Act which introduced national tests for all pupils at the ages of 7, 11 and 14. This has led some educationalists to claim that Britain has the most exam-orientated system in the world. It is certainly more so than, say, the USA or Canada but it is less so than the Soviet system, while in Japan the pressure of exams is so great, particularly for entry to higher education, that the Japanese speak of 'the examination entrance *hell*'.

The case for public examinations is simple. They are, *pace* the egalitarians, a fair and disinterested check on what the teacher has taught and the pupil has learnt, including the skill of conveying knowledge and understanding to the examiner. Exams are not subject to the partiality of teachers as continuous assessment can be. They provide a target or focus for teaching. The idea that if only there were no exams, teachers and pupils would happily engage in a series of Socratic dialogues in search of truth is nonsense. It may be regrettable that pupils will not work at a subject they do not like unless they know they are to be examined, but that is a fact of school life. Nor is it true that tests and examinations force the teacher to abandon altogether those eccentric avenues of enquiry that can bring even the dullest lesson to life. A good teacher will never teach solely for the exam, nor does the British system require him to do so.

Examination 'hell' is not an inevitable consequence of a well-examined education system. What has happened in Japan is that they have been so successful in raising the general level of education in the population that the competition to gain entry to senior high school and university has become almost unbearably fierce. That competition affects the whole system so that even some kindergartens have entrance examinations.

The stock response of the British to the Japanese education system is to ignore the successes and to highlight the psychological damage of intense competition and conformity. The Japanese are increasingly aware of the dangers of competition particularly as it affects the later stages of secondary education. Delinquency, school violence and drop-outs, as well as cases of psychological breakdown under pressure are all aspects of the same problem that worry the Japanese. But while they appear to have allowed their competitive school ethos to intensify to a degree that even they recognize as harmful, it does not mean that their basic approach to education is wrong. Nor should we dismiss their successes with slick references to anorexia and adolescent suicide. The down-side of Japan's education success should not persuade us that we have nothing to learn from the Japanese on how we should teach. It is the attitude to innate intelligence, to which I referred briefly in Chapter 3, which is fundamentally different from the attitude in the West.

Western child-centred education insists that differences in innate ability must be accommodated by an approach to teaching that is sensitive to the individual. When it comes to the all-important motivation of the child to learn, the Western approach has advantages and disadvantages. The child who believes that the teacher and the 'system' care for him or her as an individual is less likely to be discouraged by difficulty and more likely to have the confidence to say 'I don't understand.' The motivation to learn will be nurtured. But the danger of this approach is that the teacher and the 'system' may communicate to the child that their expectations of him or her are low. If there is one thing on which educationalists agree it is that most children tend to live up to or down to their teachers' expectation of them.

The Asian approach does not deny innate differences but neither does it emphasize them. The assumption is that with hard work the less intelligent can reach the same level as the more intelligent. 'Slow learners?' The official of the Japanese teachers' union looked puzzled. Then he thought he understood what his Western visitor was driving at. 'You mean child not try harder?'

As with the Western approach, the Asian has advantages and disadvantages. It encourages the teachers to have high expectations of their pupils; and it encourages the pupils to believe that they can mine their own potential, however deeply it is buried. But we in the West would argue that 'work harder' is an oversimplified response to the individual who is struggling with, say, mathematics and is more likely to reinforce his difficulties than overcome them.

It is not easy for a Westerner to be sure he understands what leads the heirs of Confucius to have such confidence that hard work can compensate for any deficiencies, or variations, in the genetic programme. I do not know Confucian philosophy but I turned to those who do and they directed me to the work of Jushichijo-Kempo, who in the seventh century gave Confucianism an ideological framework in Japan. One key phrase reads: 'While only few are born wise, it is open to many through earnest endeavour to become wise.' You may not be born with high intelligence but you can obtain the fruits of high intelligence by earnest endeavour. Or in educational terms, all can achieve high standards by hard work.

The British find this educational philosophy hard to

swallow. Working hard has always been a minority interest in British schools or, to be more accurate, in English schools. The Scots and Welsh, driven by Calvinism or by the need to fight for opportunity in a society dominated by the English, have always respected scholastic diligence and the village dominie who insisted on it.

The English are different. For generations they have pilloried and persecuted any pupil who worked hard in school, called him a swot, a mug, a muzz, a groise, according to which aristocratic public school they patronized. The sons of English gentlemen regarded academic endeavour as beneath them; the sons of the English proletariat regarded it as above and beyond them. In between, there were special schools for swots known as grammar schools, sneered at from above and resented from below. Despite the Labour Party's egalitarian rhetoric, what made possible the destruction of the grammar schools in the 1970s was that the snobs and yobs were only too pleased to see the swots put firmly in their place.

The word 'swot' to describe everything the English dislike about a mark-grubbing, ink-stained, bespectacled blackleg is derived – inappropriately – from the distortion of a Scottish accent. A nineteenth-century professor of mathematics at the Royal Military Academy at Sandhurst emphasized the difficulty of his subject by telling the cadets' 'It makes me sweat!' In broad Scots the 'sweat' became 'swot'.

Sweating or swotting: the English will have none of it. In today's comprehensives, as in yesterday's exclusive public schools, the pupil who shows too much zeal for his work is popular with neither his teachers nor his peers. In this respect, progressive education in Britain remains deeply traditional.

A somewhat similar attitude characterizes the school system of the United States (where in private schools the swot is called a 'sweat' or an 'embryo joe'). But the Americans are more aware than the British of the possible connection between the high achievement in Asian schools and the shift in world economic power to the Far East. They also have the evidence provided by an increasingly oriental immigration which enables them to see at first hand the contrast between Anglo-Saxon attitudes and the academic drive of what are called 'America's Asian whizz-kids'. In August 1987, *Time* magazine reported, 'Young Asian Americans, largely those with Chinese, Korean and Indo-Chinese backgrounds, are setting the educational pace for the rest of America and cutting a dazzling figure in the country's finest schools.'

We need to remember that behind this swot-ethic is not just immigrant ambition and family solidarity, but a fundamental belief that innate ability is less important than the individual's capacity and will to achieve. The motivation is not the same therefore as that of the British grammar school swot who believed that what held *him* back was not lack of innate ability but a class system that conferred rewards irrespective of merit.

It is unlikely that we can transplant the oriental work ethic to British schools unless we can undermine the conviction, so deeply engrained in our society, that only a few are born with brains and that the majority are not worth educating beyond an elementary stage. Our hostility towards those who work hard in school and our belief in the decisive influence of innate ability make our approach to the question of how we should teach fundamentally different from that of the Chinese or Japanese. That would not matter if we were satisfied that our methods were producing the results we wanted. But we are so dissatisfied with the results of our schooling that at the very least we should ask ourselves why the Far Eastern approach seems to be more successful. We are not able to reproduce the cultural context of their work ethic, but that does not mean it has nothing to teach us.

For a start, it should encourage us to look again at the

advantages of didactic teaching with its emphasis on rote learning and good classroom discipline. The British education establishment believes that the didactic approach is a thing of the past; the Chinese and Japanese experience suggests that it might be the British education establishment which is living in the past, clinging to the romantic episode of progressive education. However much progressives may defend their 'whig' interpretation of educational history as the story of continuous progress, the fact is that in Chinese and Japanese schools children are being taught to master subjects, notably mathematics, more effectively than in Britain and by traditional methods that we have largely rejected. In the Japanese school it is step-by-step instruction – memorize, repeat, drill, test – as laid down in the national teachers' manual.

The first lesson that the Asian whizz-kids can teach us therefore is that changes in the way we teach are not the same as improvements or *advances* in, say, medicine or aeronautical engineering. When child-centred education replaced the traditional, didactic style it was not the same type of progress as chloroform replacing whisky, or the jet engine superseding the propeller. Progressive education is not an irreversible change. I think it will turn out to have been a romantic episode. Some of its insights into the way children learn will be absorbed into a revival of traditional methods. In the primary schools, for example, I would expect there to be in the next decade a revival of *some* rote learning, greater classroom formality and use of textbooks, but not a return to the situation before the revolution, or the creation of a highly competitive ethos such as exists in Japan. In other words, the way we teach will be decided not by ideology but by common sense. If, however, dogmatism rather than pragmatism continues to dictate our choice of teaching methods, then we shall continue to sell our children short and fail to produce the well-educated population on which our prosperity depends.

The second lesson we can learn from the Asian approach is the importance of teachers having high expectations of their pupils. We know this already but seldom put it into practice. We do not expect all our children to achieve a high standard because we do not believe that most of them are capable of it. We fear that high expectations, because they are unrealistic, may be damaging to the child's confidence. Expecting the best would be the enemy of achieving the good.

The fear is not foolish; experience does suggest that setting expectations too high can undermine motivation. Where we go wrong is in allowing an atmosphere of low expectations to pervade so much of our state education system. Defeatism does not seem to be too strong a word for the attitude of some inner-city schools. Low expectations in such schools reinforce the low expectations of parents, whereas in the affluent suburbs and in many independent schools the high expectations reinforce the *high* expectations of the parents. In Britain, high expectations are part of the apparatus of privilege; in China or Japan they are available to all children.

It is easier to identify the flaw than to say how it should be corrected. But under the Education Reform Act one method is being introduced. All pupils will have to take national tests at the ages of 7, 11 and 14 to assess whether they have reached set targets in the subjects prescribed under the national curriculum. Many teachers fear these national tests will impose an arbitrary restriction on their teaching and damage the confidence of pupils who fail. I find it extraordinary that a teacher should argue that his work is 'restricted' because his pupils will be tested in two or three years' time, or that such testing will 'devalue his professional role'. The professional teacher should welcome clear short-term objectives for himself and his pupils. The bad teacher will not welcome testing because it will require him to concentrate on the task in hand, set and mark homework efficiently and use teaching methods that work, not those that reflect his social ideology. Above all, he will be obliged to have higher expectations of his pupils.

The pupils, like the professional teacher, will welcome testing. They do not fear failure as much as the adults fear it on their behalf. As in the case of competition, failure in a test only does harm to a child who does not feel valued by the school. National tests will be as much a test of the school's pastoral quality as of the efficiency of its teaching.

The third and final lesson we can learn from the Asian countries about how to teach is so obvious I hesitate to write it down. Good order is a precondition of good learning. Everyone who studies schooling in China or Japan is struck by the good order that is established in the classroom. It is not inspired by fear because the children are neither cowed nor sullen. The atmosphere in a Japanese classroom is not tense but it is formal. There are rules of procedure that pupils and teachers acknowledge. The pupils greet the teacher in the morning. When they answer a question they stand beside their desks. They listen to each other and to the teacher in silence. Even teachers who wish to adopt a less formal style nevertheless insist on what might be called the basic good manners of the classroom. This good order is achieved with classes that are larger than in Britain. The average Japanese primary school class has forty to forty-five children.

Inability to establish this degree of good order in the classroom is a continuing and seemingly intractable problem in some British schools. I am not talking about extreme cases of indiscipline such as violence used by pupils against teachers. That is serious enough, but it is exceptional. More widespread and more damaging is the failure of schools and teachers to insist on the degree of good order that makes learning possible. It is not anarchy or exceptional violence that is the principal barrier to good education but the less dramatic and more common running battle with the teacher struggling to keep at bay the continuous chatter, the restless movement, and the speaking out of turn.

The progressive approach to teaching with the emphasis on informality, on spontaneity (that is 'speaking out of turn') and on breaking down the barrier between the teacher and the child has inevitably undermined the traditional formality of the British classroom. But we should not be misled by the illusion that British schoolchildren were once as impeccably behaved as the Japanese. They seldom were. There is a streak of unruliness in the British character and 'playing up the teacher' has been for centuries a popular pastime of British schoolchildren. What is more, it is a pastime that, while it may have been disapproved of by the school, was generally regarded as healthy and normal by society.

Our ambivalence towards order and disorder in the classroom, like our ambivalence towards swotting, is a luxury we can no longer afford. If our aim is to produce a well-educated society, at least as knowledgeable and skilful as that of our competitors, we cannot take a detached view of classroom disorder that prevents children learning. We do not have to reproduce the Japanese classroom style; I doubt whether we could because that style is underpinned by a well-ordered society in which, for example, there is little petty crime.

What we can and should aim for is a much more uniform recognition of the need for good order and how it is achieved. That will not happen by accident. Nor is it practicable for the central government to prescribe a sort of national curriculum for discipline. Which means that responsibility for ensuring good order in our classrooms rests where it belongs on the head teacher. Good order in the classroom is a reflection of the whole climate or ethos of the school and this in turn reflects the character and the quality of the leadership. I know that when discipline was bad in the schools of which I was headmaster, it was because I had failed to establish a common policy on discipline with my staff, or had allowed the climate in the school to become negative, sour and niggling.

No reflection on the lessons of Asian education and how far they can apply to Britain would be complete without consideration of the popular belief that Western education encourages individuals to think for themselves while Eastern education reduces them to academic cyphers incapable of original thought. I recognize the truth in that generalization – Westminster School has produced more Nobel prize winners than Japan – but I also recognize the trap it sets for us in the West, particularly in Britain. Nobel prize winners are not the measure of an education system's worth. A few original thinkers do not, unfortunately, compensate for a badly educated population. Without improving the latter no country is likely to enjoy economic prosperity in the twenty-first century.

The question that countries such as Britain and the United States have to address is whether it is possible to match Asian educational achievements without sacrificing respect for the independence of mind that is crucial not only to the production of original thinkers but also to the survival of democracy itself. It is the same question as the one I posed in an earlier chapter on the national curriculum and I think I would give the same answer. What the Japanese have shown us is that economic success in the age of high technology requires a high level of education across the population and that this in turn requires a more authoritarian, more conformist, more competitive approach to teaching than we have been willing to tolerate. But the way the Japanese have set about achieving a well-educated population reflects cultural attitudes as well as economic imperatives. There never was a tradition of encouraging independent thought in Japanese education any more than there was in Russian education. We have that tradition. It is no longer enough in itself but we can go a long way towards emulating the Japanese approach to the question 'How should we teach?' without putting that tradition at risk.

I want to conclude this chapter by asking whether knowing how to teach is a gift, a matter of instinct and personality, or a skill that can be taught and learnt. Are good teachers born or made? Ben Jonson, who was a boy at Westminster under William Camden in the sixteenth century, recorded his gratitude to his former headmaster in verse:

> Camden, most reverend head, to whom I owe
> All that I am in arts, all that I know . . .

In the myths we build around the memory of our own childhood, 'the teacher to whom I owe everything' has a central role; to him we attribute the decisive leaps in our intellectual development; his eccentricities acquire the power of legends; even when we leave him far behind, his shadow seems to fall across our path. How formidable they are in retrospect, these great teachers of the past! It in inconceivable that they had problems of discipline or engaged in anything as sordid as public salary negotiations. They were a law unto themselves, remote from fashionable trends and disdainful of the trappings of authority that sustained their less individual colleagues.

In my own schooldays, I had the good fortune to encounter two such figures: Walter Strachan, who corresponded with Aragon and took tea with Henry Moore and to whose High Certificate French periods I can trace the origin of my awakening to literature and art; and Charles Mellows, a more complex phenomenon, who communicated a lively enthusiasm for Latin and English authors by implying that the writers and their characters were acquaintances with whom he was on more or less familiar terms. When Charles Mellows spoke of Macbeth there was always a note of personal sadness, as though they had served together as young men in Duncan's army, but had subsequently drifted apart. I cannot recall his ever having to punish a boy for misbehaviour, though he did keep a large wooden sword with which to strike a token blow at the inattentive; and he used a dirty book cupboard as a dungeon for persistent offenders. Heaven knows what the National Council for Civil Liberties would have made of it all. No doubt we were denied all sorts of fundamental children's rights, but one we did enjoy: the right to be well taught.

Above all these two men encouraged us to think for ourselves, not instead of but as well as learning by rote. They were able to combine didactic teaching with those breaks for challenge and response between teacher and pupil that are so crucial to the development of the pupil's independence of mind. We learnt things by heart, including large chunks of poetry, and we learnt the declensions of French and Latin verbs parrot-fashion. But that was only the foundation of our education. When Charles Mellows taught us *Macbeth* for school certificate (the equivalent of GCSE), we learnt Macbeth's soliloquies by heart. But the dagger that I see before me is not the only thing I remember of those lessons forty-two years ago. I remember that Mellows challenged me to think about character, to question assumptions about ambition and loyalty, to explore the power and subtlety of language – in short, to think about what I was learning, not to swallow it whole.

The mark of a good teacher is that he can encourage his pupil's independence of mind while obliging him to learn, if necessary by rote, knowledge that is essential to the subject. It is usually those outside the schools who believe that this ability to teach well is comparable to the gift of tongues: you may be born with it, you may possibly have it thrust upon you by some supernatural agency, but you can never acquire it however hard you try. At the other extreme, there are those within the schools who think that familiarity with the most recent research publications is a sure foundation for success in the classroom.

In Britain the idea that there is a body of knowledge that prospective teachers have to acquire before they are let loose in the classroom, was slow to gain acceptance. There were still many untrained teachers in state schools after the Second World War, while in the independent schools, to have studied for a diploma of education was regarded as not only unnecessary but faintly discreditable, like having a degree from a foreign university. The attitude of the independent schools was not as unprofessional as it might appear. It was based on the belief that what there was to learn about being a good teacher could only be learnt by trial and error on the job. Success depended on qualities of mind and character that no amount of teaching practice or observation could assess. Much better to be thrown in at the deep end. If you survived the first few terms you had the right qualities. If you did not, you tried another school or another profession. As for the science of pedagogy, it did not exist. There were tricks of the trade and words of wisdom passed on from one generation of schoolmasters to another but they did not constitute a subject that required specialized study.

The opposite view has been held for a long time in countries that established state education much earlier. Frederick the Great of Prussia was advocating formal teacher training as early as the 1760s. In France the religious congregations which controlled the schools, trained their teachers; teaching methods and school organization were prescribed in considerable detail in – for example – the *Ratio Studiorum* of the Jesuits and the *Reglements* of the Ursulines. When the revolutionaries took over education they naturally provided for teacher training since that was the system they had inherited. Their first experiment – and probably the first ever

131

experiment in state-organized teacher training – was in Paris in 1794/5. Men of 'good character and unquestioned patriotism' were given a four-month course of republican morality, as well as on the techniques of teaching various subjects. It was not a great success – the distinguished lecturers such as the mathematician Laplace had never taught children themselves – but it did establish the principle that teachers needed training and that the state should provide it.

No one seriously questions that principle today. But there still is argument over precisely what it is about teaching that can be taught. Is it a science of pedagogy or just tricks of the trade? Is it best carried out in a training unit or in the front line?

The most important factor in teacher training is whether those responsible have themselves had recent experience in the classroom. Teachers must be trained by teachers not by professors whose last encounter with a pupil may have been twenty or thirty years ago or by lecturers who have fled from the front line to the safety of the training college. 'Those who can, teach; those who can't, train teachers' may be glib but there is an element of truth in it. Even if the trainers were once good teachers, continued employment behind the lines has bred a staff mentality. They are out of touch. All of them, including the professors, should be obliged to spend every fifth year teaching full-time in a state school, preferably in a geographical area far removed from the ivory tower. The teachers they replace could then spend a year at the university education department or training college adding a whiff of reality to the theoretical discussions. Once that interchange between trainer and practitioner has been established, the content of the training course will take on a more practical and, from the trainee's point of view, more useful character.

I do not believe there is a science of pedagogy. Teaching is a craft. The young teacher needs to learn the technique of establishing good order or, as it is rather grandly called nowadays, 'classroom management'. He should also study the history of education and the way different countries have decided what and how to teach and how to organize the school system. As I hope this book makes clear, we have much to learn from historical and international comparisons.

The value of studying educational theory – about how children learn, for example – is less certain. It should be used as a basis for discussion, not presented as an exact science whose laws will provide the young teacher with a sure guide to his job. My scepticism about much educational theory and educational research is prompted by the suspicion that those involved are trying to transform a craft into a science, sometimes perhaps to enhance their own status. In doing this they burden teaching not only with complex or pompous jargon ('classroom management') but also with a concept of progress and improvement that teaching cannot bear.

In what sense has the craft of teaching improved since 1500 or 1900? If the effectiveness of teaching is measured by the extent to which children learn, it is difficult to see how our teaching methods can be said to be an improvement on those of the medieval or Victorian schoolmaster. Nor am I persuaded that our medieval and Victorian counterparts had less understanding of the psychology of normal children.

None of which means that a young teacher should not be made aware of the insights of twentieth-century psychology or encouraged to speculate on how teaching might be made more effective. What it *does* mean is that teaching is one of those human activities, acting is another, that does not change very much because the scope for innovation or improvement is very limited. If acting today is 'better' than it was in Periclean Athens or Shakespearean London it is only in the sense that the style is better suited to modern audiences. When actors and actresses are trained, therefore, the emphasis is on the practical – there are skills they need to learn – not on the theoretical. Teacher training should be approached in the same spirit.

Are good teachers born or made? I suspect that almost anyone can be trained to be a passable actor but that the potential to be a really good actor depends on innate qualities. My experience suggests that the same is true of teaching. Almost anyone can be trained to do an adequate job in the classroom. When as a headmaster you interview candidates for a post, you know – or you think you know – when each candidate walks in the door, whether he or she has got what it takes. But the number of candidates who really do not have what it takes is small. Even when I have been obliged to appoint a man in whom I had little confidence, I have seen him develop with professional guidance and encouragement into at least a passable teacher. But the inspiring teacher, like the two I encountered in my youth, have gifts that neither training nor experience seems able to provide.

The distinction between the adequate and the inspiring teacher brings this chapter to an end on a note of caution that is not inappropriate. When we argue about how we should teach, we need to be reminded that the method used is less important than the personality of the teacher. The impact of the teacher's personality is a subject in which educational theory and educational research have taken very little interest. That is understandable. If effective teaching depends on such unpredictable elements as the way a child responds to a particular personality it can hardly be regarded as a science. Yet we know from our own experience as pupils that it is the teacher's personality that so often makes the difference between a class that is bored and a class that is well-motivated.

The last word should be with the pupils. They know little, if anything, about educational research, but they know with the certainty of those who have suffered long that changes in teaching methods, in school organization, in educational philosophy, are not worth a box of chalk unless the man or woman standing in front of them can control the class and communicate enthusiasm. Ben Jonson understood:

What name, what skill, what faith thou hast in things!
What sight in searching the most antique springs!
What weight, and what authority in thy speech!
Man scarce can make that doubt, but thou canst teach!

6

HOW SHOULD WE ORGANIZE THE SCHOOL SYSTEM?

We should approach this question solely from a pragmatic standpoint. No ideology, political or religious, should be allowed to distract us from the main issue: if our future prosperity depends on a well-educated population, not on a well-educated elite, what school organization will enable us to achieve that goal? When we consider whether grammar schools should be reintroduced or independent schools abolished, whether City Technology Colleges should be established or the school leaving age raised, we must free ourselves from the thought that any principle is at stake. What is right is what will produce the results we need.

One way of deciding whether our school organization needs to be changed is to see where it falls short of an ideal school system designed to produce that well-educated population. The main characteristics of an ideal system would be that it was a *national* system in the sense that it was centrally directed to meet national needs; that it was so structured that the overwhelming majority of the pupils continued in education until the age of 18; that there was no division at 11 or at any other age between sheep and goats, between schools for the elite and schools for the others, yet no ideological opposition to the existence of specialized schools within the non-selective system; that it was secular and that the quality of education was such that if an independent sector existed it catered only for eccentric or minority interests.

The British system falls far short of that ideal. The national curriculum is an important step towards the creation of a truly national system but the Education Reform Act has resulted in so many different types of schools with different relationships to central or local government that it is stretching a point to describe it as *a system* at all. When you add to this complexity the fact that almost every parent who can afford to do so opts out of the system and into the independent sector, the idea of a national system is diluted even further.

Whether national or not, the present system rejects about seventy per cent of its pupils at the age of 16 and ensures that those who stay at school specialize to such a degree that it is doubtful whether even this elite can be said to be well educated. Selection at 11 has virtually disappeared but the spirit of sheep and goats lives on, and was given a fillip by the rhetoric that accompanied the Education Reform Bill. The Secretary of State might reassure the public that allowing schools to opt out of local authority control did not mean a return to selection and grammar schools, but some of his colleagues, including the Prime Minister, gave the impression that this was exactly what they hoped it would mean. Finally, while it is hard to know whether or not British education is religious, it is certainly not secular.

Depressing as that analysis may appear, it is not impossible for us to transform our school organization into something resembling the ideal. The first task is to consider the implications of making the system truly national in character. The system established by the 1944 Education Act was not national. It was a *nationwide* system of locally owned and controlled schools. The central government, representing the national interest, had almost no power to influence, let alone to dictate, what was taught or what standards pupils were expected to achieve. The 1988 Act has made the *content* of education national, but has left the ownership and control of schools in a variety of hands.

The majority of state schools will for the foreseeable future continue to be owned and run by the local education authorities. A minority of schools will exercise their right under the Act to opt out of local authority control; these so-called grant-maintained schools will be funded by central government but owned and run by their own governing bodies. In the case of former 'voluntary' schools, the governing body will be in effect a religious denomination. In addition there will be City Technology Colleges which will be independent schools, centrally funded but owned by an independent trust.

The variety of choice is intended to give the consumers, that is to say the parents, more power to influence the type of education their children receive. As a means of making schools more accountable to their immediate customers, greater parental choice is an effective tactic. But as a *strategy* for building a national system of education it is flawed. There may be an urgent need to raise standards by any means, but this tactical approach is likely to produce a patchwork of good and bad schools, not a uniformly good system that will ensure that the whole population is well educated. Nor does the experience of other countries suggest that parental choice of schools is a necessary element in creating a really efficient national system. Japan produces a well-educated population with virtually no choice of different *categories* of school offered to or demanded by parents. Even in the decentralized United States parental choice is not an issue; it is taken for granted that parents will put their children through the local high schools; the independent sector, though influential in New England, makes little impact elsewhere.

It is important to make the distinction between different

categories of schools and schools in the same category with different styles. I am all in favour of the latter because it provides choice and competition without fragmenting the national system. Japanese high schools *compete* with one another. American high schools in inner cities develop different styles to give parents a choice. East Harlem in New York (District 4 in the city's school system) is a good example of a deprived area that has breathed new life into schools by encouraging them to develop different emphases and styles. It is worth pausing to ask why the need to give parents a choice of *categories* of school figures so prominently in debates about education in Britain. I think the answer is that in this country, more than in any other, attitudes to education are coloured or, more accurately, discoloured by class and political ideology. There are those on the Left and on the Right who judge the way the school system is organized not by its ability to produce a well-educated population but by the extent to which it reflects their political aims.

In this context, parental choice becomes a red rag to the Left and an article of faith to the Right. Because the Left wishes – in the words of one of its most able intellectuals, Professor A. H. Halsey – 'to see education as an instrument in the pursuit of an egalitarian society', it is bound to see parental choice as a subversive attempt to allow a privileged minority to opt out of the egalitarian utopia. The Right rejects egalitarianism and believes that market forces are sufficient to raise the quality of education. Parental choice is therefore a defence against socialist collectivism and a means of demonstrating that the market philosophy works. In other words, both major political parties *do* allow themselves to be distracted by ideology on the question of how to create a well-educated population. The Labour Party can only think in terms of a uniform system obeying egalitarian principles; the Conservative Party can only think in terms of a fragmented and diverse arrangement of schools obeying the principle of the market. From a partisan point of view each formula is correct; from a national point of view, neither is.

The key to an effective education system is to strike the right balance of power between central and local authority. The 1944 Act gave too much power to local government. Local education authorities should be allowed to administer the school system in their area but not to frustrate the wishes of central government on fundamental aspects of education policy. The balance would be wrong if, for example, local education authorities were free to retain selective grammar schools when national policy decreed that there should be no division into sheep and goats at the age of 11. That would make a nonsense of the concept of a national education policy. At the same time, it is important that within the national system, schools should both enjoy and inspire local loyalty. The right balance, therefore, would enable parents to feel that the schools their children were attending were part of the local community, and central government could be confident that the schools were following national education policy.

The 1988 Act has shifted the balance of power in the central government's favour. It may even in time lead to the disappearance of local education authorities altogether. If state schools decide in great numbers to opt out of local authority control, there will be a critical point at which the structure of education has to change, with central government regional offices replacing local education authorities.

I do not believe this degree of centralization is desirable or likely to occur. The national curriculum has guaranteed the crucial shift in the balance of power. There may be a case for reducing the power of local education authorities still further, but not for putting the total administrative control in central hands. Certain tasks have to be done locally – ensuring that all local children have a place in school, for example – and it is better that those who carry out these tasks should be sensitive to local opinion.

I do not think many people have grasped the extent to which the national curriculum will not only change the balance of power in education but also create a sense of unity and common purpose. The danger of the national curriculum is that it might encourage the view that when the unity and common purpose are provided you hardly need a *system* of schools at all. Since all children are following the same course of study, what does it matter how many variations on the theme of school there are?

That is an attractive thought but it should be resisted. A national curriculum does not in itself make an education system national. To achieve that you must have a route through the years of compulsory schooling that is common to virtually all children. In most countries, that route is elementary, or primary, school from the age of 5 or 6, followed by junior high school to the school-leaving age of 15 or 16. When they finish elementary school, the children may compete for places at the best of the local junior highs but they are not faced with the bewildering choice of categories of schools as they are in Britain, especially after the 1988 Act. In theory, at least, there are seven different routes through secondary education in Britain: the comprehensive school that has remained under local authority control; the comprehensive school that has opted out of the authority's control; the selective grammar school that has survived despite national policy; the secondary modern school, disguised as a comprehensive, that has been forced to survive alongside; the City Technology College; the independent school as a fee-paying pupil; and the independent school as a pupil whose fees are paid by the central government under the Assisted Places Scheme.

That is not a system; it is a shambles. To create a truly

national system, I would reduce the seven routes to three. For the great majority of children, the route would be automatic promotion to one of the local high schools which take children of all abilities. I would abolish any remaining selective grammar schools. If some high schools are better than others and so have a competitive entry, that is the result of healthy and inevitable competition between schools. It is not the same as selective grammar schools which make the creation of an elite and the 'undereducation' of other children national policy. I would also abolish the Assisted Places Scheme because there can be no justification for setting up a good national system and then using public funds to allow some parents to opt out of it.

As far as the City Technology Colleges are concerned, I would have no ideological objection to the existence of some high schools that have a bias towards technology or science or modern languages, nor would I prevent them selecting their pupils on the basis of aptitude, but I would want such schools to be clearly part of the national system and not run as independent schools.

The three routes through secondary education would thus be: for most children, one of the local junior high schools; for a minority with particular aptitudes, a specialist high school within the national system; and for what I hope would be an even smaller minority, an independent school. This simplified national system is based on pragmatic arguments.

The idea of an elite created by the education system is rejected not because an elite is bad in principle, but because it is inappropriate to our present needs. In Malawi, President Hastings Banda has established in the bush an English-style 'public school' called Kamuzu Academy. Its purpose is to create an elite that will provide the cadre of senior professionals and civil servants that a developing nation needs. At first sight, Kamuzu Academy may appear to be the crazy whim of an ageing president; the compulsory Latin, uniform blazers and straw hats would set many a Western liberal's teeth on edge. Egalitarians would dislike Kamuzu on principle. But there is no principle involved. Kamuzu's elitism is good if it provides what Malawi wants and needs.

Britain's needs are the opposite of Malawi's. We have passed through the stage of needing an elite and have reached the stage of needing to raise the level of education as high as possible throughout the population. As an agricultural economy, Malawi can get by with a vast semi-educated or uneducated work-force. As an economy that can only survive by competing effectively in the market for high-technology goods, Britain needs a high-quality work-force. That is why the suggestions sometimes made on the political Right that we should revive the selective grammar schools show a total misunderstanding of the economy's needs.

It is no use abandoning the idea of an educational elite unless at the same time you ensure that the schools to which *all* children go provide a high-quality education. The comprehensive schools established after the abolition of the grammar schools in the Sixties and Seventies have not provided education of high quality. The reason is that both their creation and the ethos they were given were inspired by ideology. It was the right reform made for the wrong reason. The socialists fought for comprehensive schools not because they wanted a prosperous society but because they wanted an egalitarian one. What mattered to them was that one class did not have an educational advantage over the rest. That meant not only destroying the grammar schools, but making sure that everything associated with the grammar schools – competition, streaming, didactic teaching, even hard work – was outlawed in the new comprehensives. The socialists solved the problem of how to achieve equality of opportunity by denying it to everyone. Better that no children should have a good education than that a minority have a flying start to life. Ideology triumphed over the national interest.

The triumph of ideology in education is not of course a peculiarly British or modern phenomenon. In 1793, Robespierre presented a scheme to the Revolutionary Convention to establish 'maisons d'égalité', state boarding-schools to which all children would be sent to endure a spartan regime that would remove all traces of class and prod-uce citizens in a uniform, republican mould. The advantage of the French Revolution, however, was that the more extreme ideological ideas in education seldom had time to take root before their author was guillotined. In Britain, the ideology of egalitarianism took root in education and has not yet been eradicated.

If we approach the controversy over comprehensive and grammar schools from a pragmatic standpoint, the solution is clear. We do not want an elite, so we must not go back to a sys-tem that divides children at 11. We do want a well-educated population, so we must create a new ethos of competition and hard work in the schools to which all our children are going. We cannot guillotine the ideologues of the Left who demand that the egalitarian ethos is retained or the ideologues of the Right who demand that grammar schools should be revived, but we must reject their partisan prescriptions.

The politically motivated egalitarians exploited the ideals of the progressives to such an extent that the two approaches are indistinguishable. I have already indicated that I think the egalitarian-progressive ethos will be undermined by the national curriculum, by the system of national tests, and by reform of teacher training. I do not think it necessary to take further measures to stimulate a hard-working, competitive ethos in schools or competition between schools. Once the national curriculum and the national tests exert their pressure on schools and teachers, realism will assert itself against ideology. To go beyond this and try to stimulate schools' performance by allowing some to opt out of local authority control smacks of replacing one ideology with another. If those that opt out are then allowed to transform themselves into old-style grammar schools, ideology will once again have triumphed over the national interest.

One of the principal arguments of the Conservative Party's approach to education (as distinct from Right-wing ideology) is that the quality of education will improve if the parents, as the consumers, are given a larger say in what happens in schools. I want to deal with the role of parents in the next chapter but it is worth inserting here a note of warning. While I agree that it is desirable that the parents' voice should be heard in the way an individual school is run, it is a mistake to think that parents' interests are always the same as the national interest. It is possible, for example, that parents who were themselves educated in the egalitarian and progressive ethos of the Sixties would be opposed to the more competitive and hard-working ethos that is required in the Nineties. If that should be the case, parents should have no more power than teachers or local education authorities to frustrate the wishes of the central government.

The conflict of ideologies on how the school system should be organized is nowhere more apparent than on the subject of City Technology Colleges. For the Right, the colleges represent an extension of parental choice and a means of providing healthy competition by breaking the monopoly of the local education authorities. For the Left, they are divisive and represent an attempt to reintroduce selection under the veil of technology. The City Technology Colleges are independent schools whose initial capital costs are met by industry but whose pupils' fees are met by the central government. They are a new type of state-supported secondary school designed to bring good education with a technical and vocational bias to inner-city areas. The first CTC opened in September 1988 in Solihull and a further nineteen are planned.

From the pragmatic standpoint, an exception to the general rule that there should be one type of secondary school should be judged on its merits. Is the special school providing a form of education that the general run of schools cannot? There is no point in having exceptions just to satisfy an ideological desire to extend parental choice. When the Chinese established, after the Cultural Revolution, schools for gifted children, they presumably reckoned that these children were not being stretched and stimulated enough in the ordinary schools. The nation was wasting talent. Marxist-Leninist ideology had to bend to pragmatic common sense.

Similarly, pragmatic decisions about specialist schools have been taken in other countries. In the Soviet Union, specialist schools include – as we would expect – schools for gifted children in music, ballet, and art. But more numerous and, from our point of view, more interesting are the many foreign language schools which are highly selective and in which all or part of the teaching is in a European or Far Eastern language. These Soviet specialist schools represent a pragmatic concession to a limited form of elitism so that the education system as a whole may develop the nation's talent.

In the United States federal system there is no national policy on specialist schools but such schools exist in many cities and states. In New York City, for example, there are a number of public high schools, such as Brooklyn Tech and Bronx High School of Science, that have been allowed to develop into specialist schools for gifted children.

Neither the communist nor the capitalist world has any difficulty reconciling the idea of a non-selective schooling system with the existence of schools that provide specialist education for talented children. It is the British who find this reconciliation so hard to make. The reason is this. In the

United States, in China, in the Soviet Union, educational opportunity is too well established to be threatened by the existence of a small number of schools for high-flyers. In Britain, equal opportunity in education has a much more tenuous foothold, largely because the rich and powerful send their children to prestigious schools outside the state system. It is not surprising therefore that the National Union of Teachers condemns the City Technology Colleges as 'divisive'. Insecurity dare not contemplate exceptions.

I do not think we should let fear of reinforcing privilege and inequality blind us to the fact that even as our school system improves it still might not provide the right education for some children or the concentrated education in particular subjects that the country needs. That is *not* the same as saying that we should return to selective grammar schools. There is a crucial difference between setting out with the belief that only a minority of children are worth educating to a high level, which is pure elitism, and setting out to educate all children to a high level while recognizing that special talents and special needs may need special treatment.

It is in this context that the City Technology Colleges should be judged. Though they may have been inspired as much by an ideological belief in parental choice as by a pragmatic desire to provide education with 'an emphasis on science and technology', there is a good chance that they will develop into our inner-city equivalent of the Bronx High School of Science. What may prevent them doing so is not egalitarian hostility but their own susceptibility to the British disease of low expectation.

I would like to see central government establish other specialist schools – foreign language schools are a priority in the light of 1992 – initially on an experimental basis to test the effect on the children who attend them and on the other schools in the area. When critics of specialist schools claim

147

that any 'exception' will damage the rest of the system, one is bound to ask why this does not worry a country such as China which is so determined to improve the quality of its education or why school principals in New York 'happily' send their brightest children to Bronx Science or Brooklyn Tech.

It is only fair to add that neither West Germany nor Japan feels the necessity to have specialist schools. In West Germany there is already a degree of specialization in the general education system up to the age of 15 and clear specialization after that as the majority continue in vocational training and the minority take a more academic course to the school-leaving exam, the Abitur. Japan, by contrast, does not emphasize specialization or vocational education and is satisfied with the high level of general education that compulsory schools provide. There would be no point in having schools for gifted children in Japan any more than there would be in having City Technology Colleges in West Germany. Those needs are already met.

The best education systems may not need specialist schools. But the converse is also true. No number of specialist schools can compensate for an education system that is fundamentally flawed. I have referred a number of times to the underlying cause. The British cling to the belief that most children are not capable of learning more than a few basic skills and a smattering of knowledge. The British would deny this but it shows through clearly in their attitude to the education of pupils after the age of 16. Why we cling to this belief when the rest of the developed world has outgrown it, I am not sure. Probably, it is a mixture of our inability to cast off the spell of hierarchy and class and the fact that despite all the song and dance over the Education Reform Bill, we still have a low opinion of the value of education.

The damaging consequences of the persistence of the sheep and goats model of education is that a very low proportion of our young people are in full-time education after the compulsory leaving age of 16. On the most generous interpretation of 'full-time education' the figure is only 33%. In the United States, where the school-leaving age is 16 or 17 depending on the State, between 80% and 90% of the age groups remain in full-time education to take the high school diploma. (In the USA as in Britain the figure for the inner cities is much lower than the 'national' figure.) In West Germany, where compulsory schooling ends at 15+, 85% of the age group continue in full-time education or education plus training to 18. In Japan, where compulsory schooling ends at 15, 95% are in full-time education at 18.*

If our future prosperity depends on producing a well-educated population, the significance of these figures needs no emphasis. Better to concentrate our minds on what steps have to be taken to correct this flaw in our education system.

A common denominator in the United States, West Germany and Japan is that the 16- and 17-year-olds have been withdrawn from the labour market, and we should have to do the same. In the United States and Japan, these young people remain in schools following a broad curriculum. In West Germany, they divide between vocational training and schools preparing for the Abitur.

If we copied the American and Japanese approach, we should have to abolish both the GCSE and the A-level exam and replace them with one school-leaving exam at 18, based not on specialization in three subjects, but on proficiency in five or six subjects. That is easily said, but to implement such a reform would involve enormous logistical, not to mention

*As these figures are often the subject of debate I should give my source which is *Competence and Competition, Training and Education in the Federal Republic of Germany, the United States and Japan*, published in the National Economic and Development Office and the Manpower Services Commission, 1984.

social and political, problems. Where would we find school places and teachers for the 450,000 pupils who at present leave school at 16? How could they be persuaded that it was worth staying on at school for a further two years? What happens to the families that rely on the additional incomes of their 16- and 17-year-olds? Above all, would any political party be prepared to tackle a complex and expensive reform for which there would probably be little public support?

The West German approach would raise fewer administrative problems and would be less expensive. We already have a post-16 academic stream and this could continue, though with a broader curriculum. Again, GCSE and A-level would disappear and be replaced by a single exam at 18 in five or six subjects which must include English, mathematics, and a modern foreign language.

This is a good moment to clear up a common misunderstanding about the connection between A-levels and high standards. When it was proposed by the Higginson Committee that A-level should be broadened from three subjects to five, the chairman of the Conservative backbench education committee said: 'This seems to me a general lowering of standards because you can't do five subjects in the time allocated to three.' That is true, but it is applying the wrong yardstick. The criterion for judging standards is what you are trying to achieve in the post-16 education, which is to ensure that our most able academic students do not drop essential subjects. By that yardstick, three A-levels, however good, is in fact a *lower* standard than five or six subjects studied with a 'leaner' syllabus.

The alternative route would be a national scheme of vocational education and training on the lines of the so-called Dual System in West Germany. Under the Dual System, employers provide training and the individual States (i.e. Laender) provide further education. The young people involved are apprentices and have the status of pupils, not workers. The employer gives on-the-job and off-the-job training and this is complemented by compulsory day-release education in a further education college. The content of the training is determined by Federal authorities, while the content of the education is determined by the Laender. So the Dual System is a national system of vocational education and training, supported by trades unions as well as employers, and lasting from two to four years depending on the occupation for which the individual is training. Eighty per cent of the cost is borne by the participating firms. The Laender pays for the further education element. The burden on the Federal government is small.

Britain would be wise to adopt the West German approach. It is cheaper and simpler to introduce and its practical character would make it more acceptable to the 16- and 17-year-olds as well as to the public at large. Its disadvantage is that it requires young people to choose a career – vehicle mechanic, bank clerk, electrician – at the age of 16. Under the Japanese system the broad-based schools education keeps options open to 18.

The Japanese approach more accurately reflects the ideal of producing a well-educated population; but any British government determined to increase significantly the number of young people participating in full-time education or training to the age of 18, is bound to come to the conclusion that the West German approach is more appropriate and more politi-cally credible. The one option that Britain does not have is to do nothing.

If we assume that Britain does opt for a West German approach to post-16 education and training, the future organization of our school system will look like this:

The ages of compulsory schooling will remain 5 to 16. All children will enter their local primary or elementary school at 5 and move up without examinations to one of the local secondary schools at 11. These secondary schools – let us call them junior high schools, because it is doubtful if in our lifetime the word 'comprehensive' will lose its pejorative overtone – which will be encouraged to develop distinctive styles and to compete with one another. It is at this stage that the specialist schools will provide an alternative route for a minority of children with special aptitudes or talents.

Although 16 marks the end of compulsory schooling, it will be illegal for 16- and 17-year-olds to be in full-time employment. All pupils at 16 will be encouraged to choose one of the two routes available: the 'academic' route via senior high school – entry to which would not be automatic but on merit – to a leaving exam at 18 based on six subjects; or a vocational education and training route combining apprenticeship with further education on day-release. The aim would be to make these two routes sufficiently attractive in terms of achieving either university entrance or employment that at least 80% of the age-group decide to participate. One part of the attraction would be the payment of an allowance to those in apprenticeship as happens in West Germany. Another part would be the desire to obtain a qualification; there being no school-leaving exam at 16, those finishing at that age would have no qualification to take into the adult world. Finally, all schools and colleges in the system would be secular, neither belonging to nor being operated by a religious order or denomination.

Before we throw up our hands in horror or despair and say that such a system is not for us or that it is impracticable, we should remember that every aspect of it exists and works well in one of the three countries – the United States, Japan, West Germany – with whom we have to compete if we are to enjoy any sort of prosperity.

Independent schools

The reform of the school system in Britain cannot be considered without taking some account of the role of the independent schools. Other countries have independent schools but it is only in Britain that these schools exert such a powerful influence that they cannot be ignored.

There are over two thousand independent schools in Britain. They educate 3.5% of the 5- to 11-year-olds and 5.3% of the 11- to 16-year-olds. Of those pupils staying in full-time education to 18, that is those taking three A-levels, 23% are in independent schools. The statistics are less important than the spell that the most famous of these schools cast over the education system and over society as a whole. If Britain's independent schools present a problem that has to be solved before we can create an effective national education system, it is not because they exist but because a handful of them – the so-called 'great' schools such as Eton, Winchester, Westminster, and Harrow – could almost be said to stifle at birth attempts to make Britain a land of opportunity.

In a democratic country, schools that are independent of the state's provision must be allowed to exist. It is a waste of time arguing whether or not Britain's independent schools should be abolished. It is not an option. I would go further and say that if an independent sector did not exist it would be necessary to invent one. Much as I want to see the development of an education system that commands the loyalty of the most powerful as well as the most disadvantaged in society, I am not in favour of a state monopoly. Two hundred years ago, Condorcet put the case as clearly as anyone has since: 'Private schools are a means of correcting the defects of public instruction and of maintaining the zeal of teachers through the spirit of competition . . .' he told the French Assembly in 1792. 'If any citizen is allowed to open an education establishment the result will be that the State schools will be absolutely compelled to keep themselves at least up to the level of the private schools.'

In Britain it has been popular pressure from those parents who do not patronize the independent sector and who have seen how far their own children have been at a disadvantage, that has forced politicians to do something about raising standards in state schools. It is true that the spirit of competition has been slow to take effect. This has been partly because progressive educationalists have been successful in disarming parental anxiety but principally because the state schools have not been *allowed* to compete. While the independent schools were free in the 1970s to develop a competitive academic ethos, the state schools remained shackled by progressive and egalitarian ideas. But if the Education Reform Act makes the state schools more competitive, the advantage of having an independent sector to compete with will become more apparent.

That is a good pragmatic reason for tolerating an independent sector. Yet the unique influence that the handful of 'great' schools exert in Britain makes it impossible for me to leave the argument there. I taught at Harrow for eleven years and was for sixteen years headmaster of Westminster. I applied for the headmastership of Eton, which I regard as one of the best schools in the world. If I argue that it is in the country's interests that the role of these 'great' schools should be changed, I am not – as one former colleague put it – 'rocking the boat from the safety of the shore'. I argued this case many times in the past. Nor am I being disloyal to institutions that have given me so much. The changes I advocate are as much in the schools' interests as in the country's.

I believe that the most prestigious independent schools operate against the national interest in the following way. They encourage in society a state of mind which – for want of a better phrase – I will call 'hierarchy inhibition' that makes it much more difficult for us to achieve the high level of education throughout the population that we need. The 'great' schools are a key part of Britain's social hierarchy. Other countries have class divisions and ours are by no means the most blatant or dangerous. Compared with some Latin-American countries, Britain's class system seems remarkably benign and no one would regard incipient revolution as a characteristic of British life. But paradoxically, it is the very mildness of, one might almost say 'absence of', social restlessness that may turn out to be malignant. The trouble with the British is that they accept and enjoy the nice distinctions of social class. They love hierarchy and see nothing wrong in the deferential attitude that it breeds. I am frequently astonished at the way men and women, whose achievements are not negligible, attach such great importance to titles and go to extraordinary lengths to be presented to a minor member of the Royal Family.

To blame all this on a handful of independent schools would be ridiculous. The schools are only one of a number of institutions, including the Monarchy and the House of Lords, that provide the structure of the hierarchy. But naturally enough it is through the schools that the hierarchy most directly affects the education system. They perpetuate the view that what the country really needs is an elite and they tend to depress the expectations (both the pupils' and the teachers') in the state schools. To put it in oversimplified terms, Eton's wealth and pre-eminence tend to inhibit less privileged schools and their pupils from aiming high. What is the point of having high expectations if the hierarchy is fixed against you from the start?

The harm done by the 'great' schools, therefore, is psychological. It is not their independence that matters but their ability to 'psych' the remainder of the field. If we want to produce

155

a well-educated population, we have to find a way of breaking
that spell. Some people will argue that it has already been broken and that low expectations in state schools are the result of
other factors, such as lack of resources. Others will say that the
social hierarchy has disappeared. 'That sort of thing is over
now' is a recurring theme in British social history.

I do not attribute low expectations solely to the presence of
a prestigious independent sector but I am sure the sector
makes an important contribution. Nor do I claim that the
social hierarchy is as rigid as in, say, the 1930s, but it is still
there, the ability of its separate parts to adapt to changing
times without disturbing the whole being one of the most
intriguing aspects of British life.

My point is that despite changes, the inhibiting influence of
the hierarchy and in particular the 'great' schools, which did
not matter much in the past, now presents a serious obstacle
to the achievement of the principal aim of our education system. In other countries, at other times, prestigious independent schools are not incompatible with the development of a
well-educated population but in Britain at this time they are.
That it is the *special* role played by Britain's independent
schools that creates the problem can be seen by contrasting it
with the 'harmless' role played by the independent sector in
the United States and Japan.

In the USA, between 9% and 10% of high school students
attend independent schools. Although this is a higher figure
than in Britain, the impact of the schools on American society
is much less. There are various reasons for this. Most of the
'prep' schools, as they are called, are on the East Coast: there
are many parts of the country where it would never cross anyone's mind to send a boy or girl to an independent school. It is
impossible, therefore, for these schools to exert a psychological influence – or indeed any other sort of influence – at
national level. Everyone in Britain has heard of Eton; the

number of Americans who have heard of its equivalent, Groton, is surely very small. The arguments about privilege, so familiar in Britain, do not have a nationwide importance. The elite American independent schools are just as successful at getting their pupils into Ivy League colleges as their counterparts are in the Oxford and Cambridge stakes, but that is not a subject for heated debate in Indiana or Oregon.

The United States is, as I have said, increasingly aware that it must raise the overall level of education if it is to compete with the 'well-educated economies' of the Far East, but it does not see the independent schools as a stumbling block. The schools are just not that important in a country that is so large and diverse.

Japan's independent schools do not conflict with the country's educational aims either. During the years of compulsory schooling, that is from 6 to 15, the vast majority of Japanese children – 98% – are educated in the state primary and junior schools. It is here that the central government can ensure that the basis of the well-educated population is laid. What the independent sector does is to *supplement* this basic provision. So there are private kindergartens, private supplementary schools – we would call them 'crammers', the Japanese call them *juku* – which coach 6- to 15-year-olds, after normal school hours. Although some kindergartens, *juku*, and private senior high schools are much sought-after because they facilitate the child's successful entry into the next stage of a highly competitive system, they do not have the same impact on the state schools as do Eton, Winchester, and the other 'great' schools. With very few exceptions, the wealthy and influential parents of Japan do not automatically opt out of the state school system: they may buy as much supplementary education as they can, but their children go to the same schools as all the other children.

In neither Japan nor the United states does the indepen-

dent sector obstruct the pursuit of a well-educated population. In Britain, it does; not because it is independent but
because it is an automatic choice for parents who can afford it,
and because its most prestigious schools are national symbols
of hierarchy and lack of equal opportunity. I do not believe
that Britain will achieve the overall high level of education it
needs as long as these 'great' schools continue to play their
present role. As they cannot in a democracy be forced to
change, it appears that the only way out of the dilemma is to
improve the state sector to such an extent that, as in Japan, the
wealthy and influential parents automatically choose to send
their children to the state schools.

That is the right long-term aim, but I fear it might be *very*
long term. We could accelerate the process, however, if we
could persuade the most prestigious independent schools
either to become non-fee-paying specialist schools within the
national system *or* to restrict their entry to the post-school-
leaving age of 16 to 18, like the private senior high schools in
Japan. It will be argued that the 'great' schools are flourishing
as never before and have no incentive to change. Nor is there
any reason why their governing bodies should share my view
of what is in the national interest. Nevertheless, I am convinced that a far-sighted government, particularly one that
enjoyed the confidence of the independent sector, would be
wise to explore these possibilities. If it does not, it may well
find that its attempts to raise the level of education in Britain
are frustrated, because so much depends on whether state
schools believe that, in a hierarchical society, high expectations are realistic.

William J. Bennett, President Reagan's Secretary of Education, gave as the first characteristic of good schools: 'These
schools hold to the traditional American view that no immu-
table law dooms a child to failure simply because he or she is
born into poverty. The principals and staffs of these schools

believe they *can* make a difference.' Without such optimism we shall never achieve a high level of national education. Without the prestigious and powerful independent schools, such optimism would be much easier to inspire.

7

HOW DO WE CREATE
GOOD SCHOOLS?

It requires no expertise to know that however clear the aims and however efficient the organization of your education system, the children will not be educated to a high standard unless the schools are good. Yet how to create good schools is one of the least studied aspects of education, perhaps because it is a creative process, not one that can be explained solely in terms of policy and resources. You cannot buy good schools, though a well-funded education system will make it more likely that good schools will emerge. The key to the creative process is the quality of leadership. That is why all discussions on what makes good schools possible must in the end focus on the role of the head or principal.

A good school is a school that works. It is easy to tell when a school is not working. The pupils are not achieving what they are capable of achieving; leadership is weak; morale is low and there is no sense of direction; the teachers take no pride in their work or in the institution; incompetence and slackness are tolerated because, like the graffiti on the walls, they have been there so long they have ceased to attract attention. A bad school has lost the will to put things right.

Between the good schools and the bad schools are the schools with which most parents and teachers are familiar. They have neither sunk into apathy nor sought to rise above a defensible mediocrity. They tick over, doing some things well and some things badly, content to keep the show on the road rather than face the challenge of excellence. Were it not for the presence of some excellent schools, we should probably regard these mediocre schools as satisfactory. But they are not, either from the point of view of the pupils and their parents, or from the point of view of achieving the aims of our education system.

The first step towards creating more good schools is to give schools the maximum autonomy consistent with the need to have a national system rather than a fragmented one. Every state school should be free to develop a distinctive character by, for example, developing a reputation for excellence in a particular subject, but should not be free to contradict national policy by, for example, selecting on the grounds of religious faith. The local education authority should *administer* education in its area but should have no power to influence or curtail the distinctive character that a school wishes to develop. The only restriction on the school's freedom in this respect is national not local policy.

To achieve this, the school's head and governing body must have control of the school budget. One of the most important sections in the Education Reform Act provides for this delegation of financial responsibility to schools. In future, local education authorities will allocate resources (principally on a per capita basis) and will require schools to account for their use, but the management of the resources will be the responsibility of the school. There are some practical questions that have not been resolved – the sheer mechanics of a delegated system and the potential loss of economies of scale – but these are minor when set against the great advantages of allowing each school to set its own priorities for expenditure.

One of the chief advantages is that financial responsibility encourages realism. As a group, teachers tend to know the value of everything and the cost of nothing. So long as financial responsibility is located in some remote bureaucracy, they are free to blame their own shortcomings on the lack of resources or the wrong decision on priorities. The nearer teachers – not just head teachers and governors – can be to the point at which every aspect of running a school has to be costed, the better. If the head of science argues for an increase in his department's budget he should have to convince his colleagues whose departments will get less as a result. If the head of English claims he cannot manage without an extra teacher, he should have to answer the sceptics who reckon that their departments are under as much, if not greater, pressure. More computers this year may mean fewer new books for the library; the diversification of the sports programme may mean less money for musical instruments. Having to make the choice is one way in which a school defines what it wishes its character to be. Though there is clearly a level of public funding which makes such choices invidious rather than creative, overfunding of the education system can also be damaging. Unlimited resources can encourage those involved to 'confuse process and substance' (to borrow a phrase of Ivan Illich), to believe that more education, more subjects on the timetable, more hardware in the classroom, is the same as better teaching. Limited – not scarce – resources and financial responsibility is the formula most likely to produce good teaching and efficient management.

A second important aspect of autonomy is that the head – not the central government or the local education authority or the school's governing body – should be responsible for appointing his own teaching staff. Though teachers may be employed by the central government (as in France) or by the local education authority (as in this country) it is vital that their selection should be in the hands of the man or woman who will lead them. I see no reason why in this respect a school should not be any different from other organizations in which the achievement of goals depends on the leader's ability to create a successful team. I am a director of a national newspaper. The idea that I, rather than the editor, should be responsible for selecting a new foreign editor is ridiculous. It is equally ridiculous to expect the governors of a school to have the necessary expertise and experience to select a head of French or an assistant mathematician. The only appointments in which the governing body should be involved – other than that of head – are those of deputy head and finance officer or bursar, and even here the head's wishes should as far as possible hold sway.

The head should also be responsible for the distribution of teachers among the different subjects. It is his job to resolve the argument between the head of English and his colleagues in other departments, in other words to decide the school's academic priorities within the framework of the national curriculum. But it should be the governing body's responsibility to decide how many teachers the school can afford to employ within its budget. The local authority allocates resources. The head makes recommendations for the division of those resources between teachers' salaries and other items of expenditure such as teaching materials. The governing body makes the final decision on how the budget should be distributed. The important change is that, as in an independent school, the governing body and the head have freedom to manoeuvre within the budget.

Autonomy should also mean that the governing body and the head, not the local education authority, are responsible for deciding all those aspects of the educational programme that are not covered by national policy. The school should decide the character of its sex education course. The school should decide what steps it needs to take to counter prejudice. It is precisely because such issues are likely to be contentious that decisions about them should be taken by those who are in direct contact with the pupils and their parents, and not by those who sit in County Hall. If this leaves the local education authority as an administrative rather than a policy-making body, so much the better.

My belief in the benefits of greater autonomy for schools is not based on any ideological principle. I just think that the combination of greater central direction of what is taught and greater freedom of schools to develop their own character is the formula that is most likely to raise the overall standard of education in Britain in the present context. But I do not believe that autonomy is always necessary to the creation of good schools or that autonomy can only be achieved by allowing schools to opt out of local authority control.

The Japanese have created a high standard of schools while retaining in the hands of central government and local school boards many of the powers that I would wish to see exercised by individual schools. There are good schools too in France and the Soviet Union, despite the French bureaucracy's control of all teacher appointments, and the flood of directives from Moscow that regulate almost every aspect of Soviet school life. The tradition in these countries is to rely on strong central control to create good schools. The British tradition is to rely on school autonomy.

But the British approach before 1988 represented the worst of both worlds. The central government had virtually no power to regulate what went on in schools, nor did the schools have the freedom to develop their own distinctive character. The local education authorities could frustrate the wishes of both. As a result there was diversity where uniformity was needed (that is in national policy) and uniformity where diversity was needed (that is in the character of schools available in a neighbourhood). I have oversimplified to make the point. I realize that some local education authorities ran their schools on a loose rein, and that some schools were both innovative and distinctive despite the restrictions on their autonomy. But the point is still valid. The system restricted school autonomy without any compensating gain of national uniformity.

This situation was radically altered by the Education Reform Act 1988. The power of the central government was greatly increased and financial delegation at last gave individual schools greater autonomy. But instead of reducing the power of local education authorities still further, by removing the influence of the local inspectorate and excluding local authority representatives from schools' governing bodies, the Act took the ideological and unnecessary step of allowing some schools to opt out of local authority control.

I have already mentioned East Harlem in New York City. Once regarded as the worst school district, it has been revitalized by giving individual schools the freedom to decide their own style, their own 'theme' curriculum, their own distinctive ethos. They now specialize in a range of 'themes' from science and technology to the performing arts. This in turn means that parents have a choice, not between different categories of school but between different types of school in the same category – the junior high school. The improvement in standards of work, behaviour, attendance, and teacher morale has been remarkable and this has been achieved *without* giving schools a legal right to opt out of local authority control.

Allowing schools to opt out of local authority control is another example of how a good intention (to give schools greater autonomy) can have a bad result (the fragmentation of what should be a *national* school system), if ideology dictates the means.

Critics of greater autonomy argue that while some schools may seize the opportunity to forge ahead, schools with a lacklustre governing body and poor leadership will fall further behind. That may well happen, but creating good schools is not the same as commanding a convoy; you do not have to proceed at the pace of the slowest ship. What you do have to do is to complement greater autonomy with a drive to improve the quality of leadership.

In a school, the head must be the leader. He or she cannot do the job effectively if the governing body or the parents try to do the job instead. Under an earlier (1986) Education Act, the governing body of a state school must make an annual report to parents and to follow this up with a parents' meeting at which the governors can be questioned about the school's policy. That is a good example of how things should *not* be done. The Conservative Government, in its enthusiasm to make schools accountable to parents, undermined one of the most important characteristics of a good school: the clear understanding that the head is the chief executive and that it is his or her job to report to parents and answer their questions.

The Government has undermined the concept of the head as chief executive still further. From September 1988 governors have had a right to be involved in all staff appointments and dismissals, and the number of parent-governors has been increased from two to five. Both measures reflected public dissatisfaction with the way schools have been run. Whether such measures are really necessary to the creation of good schools or are, on the contrary, antipathetic to that process, was a question that few people stopped to ask. The bandwagon of parent power had gathered an apparently irresistible momentum. The experience of the independent sector, where governors and parents do not exercise these powers, was ignored.

The independent sector itself remains curiously – some might say irresponsibly – silent on this issue. That governors, whether parents or not, should have a say in the appointment of staff is anathema to the heads of independent schools. Yet the heads' organizations, such as the Headmasters' Conference, raised not a whisper when a Conservative government imposed this requirement on the state schools.

One of the strengths of the independent schools is that the governing body respects the authority of the head. Governors are interested in the school and concerned for its welfare (they are often former pupils), they are ultimately responsible for the education programme and the financial planning, but they do not regard it as their job to be actively involved in the school's management. Their role is non-executive. If they are parents, it is by accident, not by design.

The governors' lack of personal involvement in the school is their greatest asset. A school needs a governing body to be disinterested, so that the governors can retain that sense of proportion that so easily eludes those whose emotions are engaged.

The 1986 and 1988 Education Acts clearly indicate that the present Government takes the opposite view: the more governors there are who have a personal stake in the school, the better. So the governing body of a typical state school of 600-plus pupils will now include five parent governors and two teachers' representatives as well as the five governors nominated by the local education authority and the six 'public interest' governors co-opted by the others. The head may be a member of the governing body or not, as he or she chooses.

This composition reflects the Government's view that the governing bodies of state schools *should* get involved in the management of the school, if not on a day-to-day basis, then certainly more regularly than is the case in the independent sector. It is not just a question of taking part in the appointment of teachers; state school governors are also required to deal directly with parents; to have a view on the content of the curriculum; and to advise the head on discipline. By contrast the governors of independent schools seldom deal directly with parents and regard both the curriculum and discipline as within the head's domain.

It may be asked what there is for the governing body of an independent school to do. Financial issues play a major part on the agenda, as do policy decisions on – for example – new facilities or the expansion of numbers. At its quarterly meetings, the governing body will also receive a report from the head and will raise questions and make comments. Of course, it is not always as neat and tidy as that. There was a head who managed to introduce co-education without consulting his governors, and a governor who demanded the right to beat a pupil who, mistaking the governor for a tourist, told him in blunt language to leave the premises. But for the most part the distinction between the chief executive and the board is strictly maintained: the governing body appoints the head and oversees his work; the head runs the school and reports to the governing body. If you blur that distinction by requiring governors to participate actively in the running of the school, you will also blur the source of leadership and authority. That is why I believe that as far as the role of governors is concerned, the independent sector has got it right and the Government has got it wrong. The chances of creating a good school are diminished if the head is forever having to say to the staff and the pupils, 'I'm afraid that is not my decision.'

I doubt whether many parents wish to be involved in running schools. Parents want access to the staff who teach their children; they want to be fully informed about school policy and about routine procedures for such matters as subject choice and careers guidance; and they want to know that if they have a complaint it will be fully considered and answered. Unless they are unreasonable, they do not expect the school to chop and change its policy to meet every parental demand. A friend of mine holidaying in the highlands of

Scotland telephoned the cinema in a remote community to find out what time the programme started. 'What time were you thinking of coming?' was the reply. There are parents who expect schools, too, to adjust their programmes to the individual customer, but most parents understand well enough that unless the customers are in remarkably short supply, that is not possible. What they do expect is that the head and his staff are professionals who can be trusted to hold a proper balance between the needs of the child and the interests of the school.

It may be argued that it is precisely because that trust is rare in state schools that more parent governors are necessary. But my guess is that more parent governors will tend to make matters worse. Because they have been elected to represent the parents, they will think it is their duty to quiz the head on the sort of day-to-day issues that concern them but that are not the province of the governing body. That will cause friction rather than trust. Once the governors start discussing where the pupils are going to eat their packed lunches or why biology has to be timetabled on a Friday afternoon, they have lost their way. In my experience, heads and teachers need the stimulus of a lively, interested and critical parent body. But to give parents a statutory role in the government of the school distracts the governing body from its main task and tends to undermine the chief executive on whose leadership so much depends.

In other countries, a close relationship between school and home does not have to rely on parents playing a role in the running of the school. In Japan, each school has a parent-teacher association but parents have no direct influence on the way the school is run. Yet the close cooperation between home and school is an outstanding feature of the Japanese system. Parents are officially invited once a month to watch their children in the classroom. Once every quarter, parents have an opportunity to discuss their child's progress with teachers. Teachers make a point of visiting each pupil's home to meet the parents at least once a year; and parents are given the telephone numbers of their children's teachers and are encouraged to call if there is any special problem.

That degree of cooperation between home and school is alien to the British tradition because the roots of mutual suspicion between teachers and parents are very deep. They probably have their origin in the attitude of the Victorian public schools, most of which were boarding schools that kept parents at arm's length. When a system of state schools was started in 1870, there was no tradition of cooperation between home and school to draw on. Perhaps we should not be surprised that in our time the motive for giving parents more power in education is not to improve cooperation between home and school, but to mobilize consumer dissatisfaction in the battle to raise standards.

I am convinced that giving parents a role in school government is more likely to depress standards than to raise them, more likely to delay than encourage greater cooperation between home and school on the lines that the Japanese have so successfully developed, more likely to persuade governors to discuss minutiae than to concentrate on questions of broad policy, more likely to make heads cautious than enterprising. The key to the creation of good schools is not more power to the parents, but more power to the head.

The role of the head

The headmaster or headmistress of a school needs both the qualities of a successful manager and the qualities – in however muted a form – of a 'great leader'. The Victorians would have emphasized the latter: the power to influence others, to inspire personal loyalty, to articulate and personify the values of the institution, qualities that are correctly called charismatic because they seem to be the gift of the gods. In the late twentieth century, we are suspicious of charismatic leadership, regarding it as irrational, even at times insane. We prefer our leaders to be managers, well versed in the science of administration and confident that problems can be solved by reason.

Much of what a head does could be described as managerial, but I do not believe that good management alone creates a good school. A school is an odd institution; it has to 'work' simultaneously for a 13-year-old pupil and a 50-year-old teacher, and whether it works for either depends as much on intangible factors such as the ethos or spirit of the place as on the application of reason to management problems. Of course there are intangible factors in the success or failure of most enterprises but they are particularly important in a school where every aspect of the operation is concerned with human behaviour. This strange community of adults and children needs at least a touch of charismatic leadership if it is to develop the sense of common purpose that will enable it to achieve its goals.

Sister —— is principal of one of the largest state comprehensive schools in the country. She is shrewd, kindly, resilient and realistic. She has an authority that appears to be natural because it requires neither ritual nor posturing to sustain it. Her style is in contrast to that of the Victorian headmasters who strode about, striking awe into pupils and staff, even into their own wives. 'I remember', wrote the widow of one of Australia's Victorian headmasters, 'I felt it rather an honour, a privilege, to press his trousers.'

Today, the Victorian version of charismatic leadership would only succeed in reducing pupils and staff, not to mention wives, to uncontrollable mirth. Yet the phenomenon is still present, the heads of good schools in both the state and the independent sector seeming to possess a dimension to

171

their leadership that has nothing to do with good management. Sister —— runs a school in a deprived area of an inner city, yet her school has all the hallmarks of excellence: high morale, unostentatious efficiency, liveliness and good order. She has created the intangible ethos or spirit that brings out the best in the youngest pupil and the oldest teacher. Do not ask me how it is done. I doubt whether it is consciously 'done' at all; it is a reflection of her personality and of her commitment to the school.

If successful leadership in schools depends largely on an aspect of personality that is difficult to define, it is at first sight unremarkable that the selection of heads should be such a hit-and-miss affair. Though my experience of this has been in the independent sector, I have no reason to believe that it is any different in the state sector because the methods used are essentially the same. The governing body draws up a short list of applicants and makes the selection principally on the strength of an interview.

It is right that the governing body should make the selection, but wrong that they should rely so much on their own judgement and on a method – the interview – that can be so misleading. Those whose profession it is to help organizations find the right chief executive insist that the most unreliable method of selection is interview by a committee. Everyone on a selection committee is convinced that he or she is an excellent judge of character. Even that delusion would not matter so much if every candidate on the short list were capable of doing the job. But there is usually only the most superficial attempt to analyse what the school's needs are and what qualities and experience the governors should be looking for. It is common practice, for example, for the governors to rely on the recommendation of referees nominated by the applicant. One of the most famous independent schools appointed a new headmaster without checking on his performance as headmaster at his previous school. The man had not given a referee from that school and the selection committee had not thought to ask. The previous school was delighted to be rid of him and the new school soon regretted their choice.

Governing bodies are very reluctant to seek professional advice in the selection of heads. The selection process makes them feel important and gives them an opportunity to exercise their power. Whether it is a bishop expressing doubts about a candidate's doctrinal soundness or a left-wing councillor questioning a candidate's ideological purity, the pleasure of giving the kiss of death to an application is the same. The only way to prevent personal prejudice and delusions of perspicacity saddling the school with an inadequate head, is to use professional help in drawing up the short list. Professionals can be more thorough and more objective in analysing the school's needs and in matching potential candidates to them. If the techniques of executive search can be applied to so many other fields, they can be applied to education. There is also a wealth of expertise and experience available for assessing the qualities of personality that a candidate will bring to the job. It may be impossible to pin down the essence of charismatic leadership but there are well-tried methods for checking how well an individual performs under pressure. Some heads are at their best only when the going gets rough and may even welcome crises in order to motivate themselves; other heads are good at maintaining the rhythm of a well-oiled operation but are thrown by the unexpected. If the school needs radical reform, it is useful to know that you have the right personalities on the short list.

Amateurism in the selection of heads is matched by a perfunctory approach to professional training. Neither the state nor the independent sector takes the matter very seriously. In other areas of national concern – defence, for example – we would be appalled if senior command were given to men who had had no formal training. Promotion to senior rank in the army depends on the successful completion of the staff college course. Yet we give senior command in our school system to men and women who have no comparable qualification. If the creation of good schools depends on the quality of leadership, we cannot leave it to chance that individuals such as Sister —— will appear. The majority of heads are not in that class but they would be better at their jobs if they had been required to attend a staff college for head teachers.

The idea of using executive search methods and of establishing a staff college will seem to have little relevance to those schools that have difficulty finding *one* credible candidate for the post of head. It is in the state sector that the head's job is increasingly difficult to fill. But even in the independent sector where heads have more autonomy and authority, less stress and better remuneration, a number of governing bodies have had to re-advertise because the quality of the field was so poor.

As far as the state sector is concerned, the reasons for the shortfall are obvious. The head faces an increasingly complex and unpleasant task without proper training, with diminishing authority, and for low pay. The total remuneration of the head of an independent school can be *double* that of a head in the state sector. If we want our state schools to produce a well-educated population, we shall have to improve not only the training and the authority of head teachers but also their rewards. They are the Secretary of State's front-line managers; unless they are of high calibre, the best-laid plans to raise the overall standard of education will go astray.

The justification for placing so much emphasis on the role of the head is that schools are peculiarly sensitive to good and bad leadership. There are very few schools whose traditions are so robust that they can ride out a period of incompetence and weakness at the top. The rise and fall of schools' fortunes under different heads is such a commonplace phenomenon that it is hardly worth remarking on. Is there any other institution in which the impact of the leader is so immediate and so pervasive?

By design or default the head dictates the values of the school. Whether he likes it or not, his decisions, his priorities, what he praises and condemns, will become the currency of the institution. They are not the only values the pupils will encounter; the values of their home will be much more influential than those of school, and even in school there are two sets of values operating, those of the adults and those of the pupils' underworld. But the values the head chooses to emphasize are an essential part of the pupils' education as well as being the principal means by which he creates the spirit or ethos of the community.

'Values in education' is a subject that philosophers and sociologists complicate unnecessarily. It is not the school's job to speculate on whether values have any metaphysical validation or whether this or that value is 'middle class'. The values that a school should stand for are obvious to anyone who is not inhibited by philosophical doubts or class-conscious anxieties. They are commonsense, Clapham omnibus values. What is more, they are the values of any civilized society. So the school cannot be seen to prefer lying to truthfulness, self-indulgence to self-control, bigotry to open-mindedness, laziness to diligence, selfishness and cruelty to consideration for others, moral cowardice to moral courage.

The head, by his or her words and actions, must uphold these values, and by leadership encourage staff to uphold them too. There is no way that heads can escape this most important aspect of leadership; whether they take a stand against stealing, for example, or shrug their shoulders at the impossibility of preventing it, they are engaged in the moral education of their pupils.

175

There are those who argue that moral education should be part of the curriculum but I am convinced that it is only from the leadership of the head that the school community takes its moral values, its sense of what is right and wrong in human behaviour. In nineteenth-century France, republican education attempted to teach morality with constantly revised textbooks and maxims to learn by heart such as 'Ingratitude is a form of treason', but it was widely acknowledged to be a failure. In modern Japan, moral education is part of the compulsory curriculum but it does not relieve the head of the responsibility of moral leadership. It is common practice in Japanese schools for each Monday morning to begin with an assembly of the whole school, at which the principal gives a short homily to point a moral lesson from some incident that has occurred in the life of the school. Upon the head the tone (to use an old-fashioned word) of the school depends.

The quality of the head's leadership will also dictate the quality of his staff. He should select them but whether he does or not – and even at the end of his career there will still be some he has inherited – he is responsible for bringing out the best in them. They are a curious mixture. Some have a vocation in the sense that they would rather teach than do anything else in the world. Some have dropped into teaching when their more exalted aspirations were disappointed. Some have drifted into teaching because no other avenue appeared to be open to them. No doubt this is true of other jobs, but it seems to be especially true of teaching. Perhaps the mixture accounts for the contradictions that come to mind when trying to describe what teachers are like. They are both individualistic and dependent. They are sensitive to criticism yet in need of reassurance. They have rejected the rat race but they are acutely conscious of their own financial position. They want to be regarded as professionals while seeming to resent any attempt to assess their performance.

The contradictions make the head's role both crucial and difficult. Teachers are not easy people to lead. The difficulty is increased by the unusual nature of a career in teaching. A competent teacher may never achieve promotion, may not even seek it, and may at the age of 65 be teaching exactly the same topic in physics or history as he taught forty years earlier when his career started. What is remarkable about some teachers is that they retain their freshness and enthusiasm to the end. Those who do not present the head with the problem of motivating staff in its most acute form.

In so many other careers, those who have given their best can be moved sideways into less demanding and less important jobs. But there are no such jobs in teaching. The wealthier independent schools can afford to give their tired teachers a token timetable, but in the state sector the teacher who has lost interest must earn his pay in the classroom until the day he retires. For the children and their parents it is irrelevant that he may once have taught brilliantly; if he fails to teach them well now, they may never get a second chance to learn. From their point of view, the sooner he is replaced, the better. But from the point of view of the teacher, early retirement means his already meagre pension will be reduced.

I think it was Eric Linklater who recalled seeing this notice in the window of a New York funeral parlour during the Depression: 'Why walk around half-dead when we can bury you for seven dollars fifty?' Faced with a teacher who is going through the motions while waiting for retirement, the head may wish he could make a similar offer; but there are no cheap funerals and certainly no golden handshakes in school-teaching. The head is expected to motivate the half-dead teachers as best he can.

Such teachers are part of a wider problem of how heads should deal with incompetence. If I dwell on this problem, it is not because I think most teachers are incompetent but

177

because this issue, more than any other, preoccupies the head and because it raises the important and contentious question of how the work of teachers should be assessed.

No one knows how widespread the problem is. The view of the Department of Education and Science is that 'a significant number of teachers are performing below the standard required to achieve the planned objectives of schools'. Bad teachers do not have tenure but they are protected by the teachers' unions and by the head's reluctance to take action. They are also protected by the spurious claim that teaching is different from all other jobs in that it is so subtle and complex you cannot tell the good teachers from the bad. 'There is no guarantee', the National Union of Teachers argues, 'that objective criteria could be drawn up and applied to assess the best classroom teachers.'

The outside world is not convinced. Whether children learn anything worthwhile will strike most people as an objective criterion. Pupils' results in tests, whether of basic literacy or A-level physics, may not be the only criterion of a teacher's competence, but they are one objective criterion nevertheless. If pupils cannot complete a job application form correctly after eleven years of compulsory schooling, society is entitled to ask whether the teachers responsible are fit for the job. And every head knows who are the competent and the incompetent teachers on his staff. There really is no mystery about what constitutes good and bad teaching.

Yet some heads, faced with powerful unions, are reluctant to dismiss incompetent teachers. The law requires proof of incompetence and without a national programme of teacher assessment, such proof is hard to obtain. Pilot projects for such a programme are under way in different parts of the country, but they are regarded with deep suspicion by the NUT. The Union believes that assessment should mean self-evaluation and discussion with a colleague on professional development. It is opposed to any form of assessment that is used to identify bad teachers and promote good ones. It is also opposed to the head checking on the competence of his staff: 'The Union is not convinced that formal assessment of teachers' classroom performance by head teachers and senior staff . . . is necessarily desirable.'

Whatever system of assessment is introduced, the burden of responsbility must fall on the head and he must have the power, within the law, to dismiss those teachers who 'are performing below the standard required'. The United States Department of Education has recently published a record of how schools in the most disadvantaged areas pulled themselves out of the gutter and gave their children hope. It is striking how often the answer was to give the head effective responsibility for his staff. A high school principal in Washington DC, for example, transformed the school by insisting that he should 'evaluate all staff members and improve or replace low-performing personnel'.

On the question of improving the performance of staff, I am in favour of giving the head authority to make merit awards in the form of additional salary on a year-by-year basis. I am not suggesting that this should be a substitute for leadership; praise may be as effective a motivator as extra cash. And I am not thinking of the high-flyers who are going on to become heads of departments and head teachers. Some American states have the title of 'master teacher' which is recognized in the pay packet. My idea of a master teacher is a man or woman who can work wonders with the bottom sets, who can motivate the pupils who have been defeated, who have high expectations of the least able, and who can turn those high expectations into the qualifications that the pupils need.

I would also give the head authority within the budget and with the approval of the governing body to offer differential salaries to attract teachers in those subjects where expertise is in short supply. The teaching profession does not like the idea of paying a mathematician more than a historian, but the laws of supply and demand dictate that we should.

I have argued that the creation of good schools depends on giving the head both the responsibility for running his school and the authority to do so effectively. The more he has to share his executive authority with governors, the longer incompetence is likely to be entrenched. The governors should not usurp the head's authority; they should make sure he uses it.

The pupils are often more perceptive than the staff when it comes to identifying where the real power lies. They know what struggles are going on and who wins and who loses. If the head is seen to be without effective authority, he will find it that much more difficult to command the respect of his pupils; and upon that respect the discipline of the school is based. Just as the values of the school, its intangible ethos or spirit, as well as the quality and performance of the staff, depend crucially on the head's leadership, so does the discipline or lack of it. If the local education authority or the governors reinstate a pupil the head has suspended, discipline is undermined. Those who appoint the head presumably believe that he can do the job. If it turns out that he cannot, he should be replaced like any other member of staff. What should never happen is that his authority is undermined by those who appointed him.

I have made the head's position sound an embattled one, a series of confrontations with interfering governors, critical parents, hostile unions, incompetent staff, and indisciplined pupils. That may not be the whole truth but it is not a caricature of the head's life either. The stresses and the hard knocks emphasize how important it is to get the selection, the training, the responsibilities and the rewards of heads right. It is arguable that in state schools at the moment they are all wrong; which is one reason why the shortage of good candidates for the job poses as serious a threat to the success of educational reform as the shortage of qualified teachers in mathematics, science, technology, and modern languages. The specific steps the central government should take are: to give heads effective authority comparable to that enjoyed by heads in the independent sector; to establish a staff college course that all prospective heads have to pass; and to increase the remuneration of heads to at least the level of the independent schools.

We are not going to achieve a well-educated population unless we create good schools. The creation of good schools depends primarily on the quality of the head's leadership. We cannot, therefore, leave the emergence of good heads to chance.

CONCLUSION

TOO LITTLE TOO LATE?

The history of educational reform in Britain is the history of missed opportunity. It is not that the reforms have been mistaken in concept or ineffective in operation; the opportunities have been missed because the reforms have never fully matched up to the needs of the country at the time. Thus in 1870 when W. E. Forster clearly recognized that 'upon the speedy provision of elementary education depends our industrial prosperity', the Act that bears his name fell far short of establishing the national system of elementary education that the country needed. In 1944, when it was equally clear that Britain's changed circumstances demanded a secondary education system geared to economic recovery, the Butler Act failed to acknowledge this fact or to give the central government any effective say in what was taught in schools.

The missed opportunities reflected both the need for political caution and compromise and the inability to read the signs of the times correctly, a failing common to all great powers in their period of decline. It would have required a Peter the Great to force the British in 1870 or even in 1944 to accept a reform that would have been as much against the grain of tradition as a national curriculum.

At first sight the Education Reform Act of 1988 is more in the style of Peter the Great than of W. E. Forster and R. A. Butler: radical rather than tentative; based on conviction rather than on consensus. But on closer scrutiny it has some of the familiar characteristics of a missed opportunity. It goes so far but not far enough to meet the country's needs, and it contains some reforms that may work against the needs rather than for them.

The principal need is for a well-educated population instead of an educated elite and an undereducated mass. If there are still politicians or educationalists who have not grasped this point it is because they, like their predecessors in 1870 and 1944, have failed to read correctly the signs of the times. Economic prosperity upon which all else depends – security, social services, social cohesion – will in the future have to be based on a high-quality work-force. Those who doubt that proposition should read Paul Kennedy's *The Rise and Fall of the Great Powers*, and in particular that section that analyses the reasons for Japan's economic pre-eminence.

It is probably more difficult for Britain than for any of her competitors to accept this change of emphasis in the education system. There are deeply entrenched national attitudes that inhibit change. The belief that only a minority is worth educating beyond a rudimentary stage is still strongly held; and it is in re-enforcing this belief that the existence of prestigious independent schools does so much harm. Elitism worked well for Britain in the past but it is fatal to the country's future.

Suspicion of central government's direction is also deeply rooted in the British character. It would have been unthinkable for W. E. Forster to echo the sentiment of his contemporary in Japan, Mori Arinori: 'Education is not for the sake of the student but for the sake of the state.' In the twentieth century, the central government has extended its control over many aspects of British life but in education the British have remained hostile to the idea that a government minister should tell schools what to teach.

It is the persistence of these attitudes that partly accounts for the ambivalence and contradictory nature of the 1988 Act.

Another factor that has contributed to the contradictions in the Act is that so much educational change in Britain has been inspired not by the national interest but by political ideology. I can think of no other country in which the school system has been chopped and changed so often to suit party political doctrine.

Any attempt to assess the virtues and limitations of the 1988 Act must therefore keep these factors in mind. Neither Kenneth Baker nor the Department of Education and Science had a free hand to introduce the reforms they may have deemed necessary to meet the country's needs. Having said that, the yardstick for judging whether they seized or missed their opportunity remains the degree to which the provisions of the Act are likely to produce a high level of education throughout the population.

The position when the Act became law was that Britain had probably the worst-educated population of any industrialized country. In those subjects that are testable, notably mathematics, international comparisons show British children far behind their contemporaries in West Germany and Japan. Vertical comparisons with British children in the past are irrelevant. More serious and more damning, because it is deliberate policy, Britain is alone among industrialized countries in dismissing over three-quarters of its school pupils at 16. This is not a function of the school-leaving age – it is lower in Japan – but of the traditional belief that education beyond that age is for an academically minded minority only. Britain is already short of skilled workers; as it has to invest more of its future in high technology, that shortage will become acute. The necessary level of education is just not there.

So the critical question is: How far will the 1988 reforms go towards transforming a largely under-educated population into a well-educated one?

184

The first thing to say is that the introduction of the national curriculum is the most important reform in the history of British education. It brings to an end a century of *laissez faire* education and in doing so it signals that for the first time the British recognize the connection between schooling and national prosperity, and acknowledge that education is not only in the interests of the student but also in the interests of the state.

The national curriculum cannot help but improve the standard of education in this country. It will also provide the opportunity 'to ensure that all children understand the language, history and cultural values by which our society was formed'. And the series of tests that will check how effectively the curriculum is being taught will go a long way to eradicate the sillier, progressive and egalitarian ideas.

The potential effect of the national curriculum is enormous. There have been and will be attempts to reduce its impact, particularly by weakening the prescriptive element. The right-wing Centre for Policy Studies has never liked it and tried to have it truncated when Sir Keith Joseph moved an unsuccessful amendment to that effect in the Lords. Left-wing ideologues are equally strongly opposed to the idea of the curriculum teaching all children a common cultural heritage. The cornerstone of the Act may yet be threatened by the political ideology that has bedevilled British education since the war.

Much of the rest of the Act, as it applies to schools, is designed to raise standards by giving schools greater autonomy and by bringing parents into more active partnership with the teachers. Both these policies could contribute to a better-educated population but where they bear the stamp of ideology rather than of the national interest they are less likely to do so. The delegation of financial responsibility to schools should make them more efficient and more disposed to develop a distinctive ethos; allowing schools to opt out of local authority control could have the same effect but it will fragment the national system in a way that no other country with a successful education system thinks desirable and could encourage the return of the grammar school mentality which is not in the country's long-term interests. Similarly, parent-teacher cooperation on the Japanese model would undoubtedly raise standards, but parent power on the British model, with parents' representatives having power over teachers, will make cooperation more difficult and will undermine the authority of the head on whom the creation of good schools depends.

The City Technology Colleges exemplify what is good and bad about the Act. Specialist secondary schools work well in some other countries and it would have made sense for the Act to provide for the setting up of some specialist schools as part of our national system. But ideology dictated a different approach. Instead of justifying the schools in terms of the country's need for specialist skills – linguists, engineers – the justification was expressed primarily in terms of the right wing's preoccupation with parental choice. Instead of making the specialist schools part of the national system, it was decided that they should be independent schools, partly funded by industry. From the start a good idea for contributing to a better-educated population was discredited in the eyes of many who would have supported it because it was seen to be the child of ideology. There is no reason why a policy inspired by political ideology should not also be in the national interest but it will not win general support if it is presented in terms of the former instead of the latter. The Labour Party failed to win support for tackling the problem of the independent schools because its policies were seen to be motivated by political ideology.

The City Technology Colleges may prove successful despite their origins. I hope they do, not least because they will expect parents to commit themselves to the idea of children staying in full-time education or training until the age of 18. But how much better it would have been if the Colleges had been conceived as national assets, not as exemplars of a political doctrine.

The 1988 Act should also be judged, like its predecessors, by what it has failed to do. No Education Act can be expected to deal with every problem but a major Act such as this must address the key discrepancies between what the nation needs and what the education system is delivering. We need a well-educated population from which to draw a high-quality work-force. What the education system delivers is an under-educated population. The national curriculum addresses this discrepancy. In doing so it has dealt what is, I hope, a fatal blow to the British belief that the central direction of education is incompatible with democracy.

But the 1988 Act has not dealt a fatal blow to the other anachronistic British belief that there is only a minority of pupils worth educating beyond 16. We should not be surprised that we have an undereducated population; that is precisely what our education system is designed to produce. It is this fault that the 1988 Act fails to tackle. Not only does it give succour to grammar school buffs. There is nothing in the Act, apart from the City Technology Colleges, to increase the proportion of the age-group continuing in education or training after the school-leaving age. There is no attempt to introduce a Dual System as in West Germany or to broaden the sixth-form curriculum or to prevent 16- to 18-year-olds entering the labour market. A government committee, the Higginson Committee, set up to consider the future of A-levels, reported while the Education Reform Bill was in parliament and recommended that the sixth-form curriculum should be broadened. As we have seen, the recommendation was rejected by the Government.

It would appear from the 1988 Act and from the rejection of the Higginson recommendation that the Government either does not agree that our future prosperity depends on having a well-educated population *or* believes that such a population can be obtained despite the fact that three-quarters of our young people leave education at 16.

If either is true, then 1988 will confirm what has already been suggested by 1870 and 1944: the history of educational reform in Britain is the history of missed opportunity. I find it hard to believe that a politician as astute and pragmatic as Kenneth Baker does not recognize as clearly as did W. E. Forster in 1870, the direct connection between education and economic prosperity. But as Forster discovered, persuading your colleagues to accept the implications may take a long time. What Forster wanted – a publicly controlled national system of elementary education – did not become a reality until 1944. The revolution in British attitudes to education started by Baker in 1988 cannot wait three-quarters of a century to be completed. And completion means above all dealing that fatal blow to the elitist notion that education after 16 is for academic specialists only.

The 1988 Act *was* incomplete and the one major reform it introduced – the national curriculum – *was* overdue. As I have argued throughout this book, there are many other changes that are necessary. I do not expect everyone to agree with my diagnosis of what is required but I do believe that the issues I have raised – whether they are fundamental issues such as the need to be clear about the aims of the education system or practical issues such as the need to strengthen the training and authority of head teachers, or contentious issues such as the need to confront the harm done by the independent schools – are the ones that cannot be ignored.

Yet, while 'too little too late' may be an apt comment, it is too final and pessimistic a note on which to conclude this personal critique of the state of British education. I must at least express the hope that the combined effect of the national curriculum and an increasing national awareness of the role of education in other nations' economic success will persuade the British that the 1988 Act should be seen as only the first step in a process of radical educational reform.

One day we may have a truly national education system of which we can be proud and of which other countries are envious. If this book has done anything to encourage discussion of how we reach that day from where we are now, I shall be satisfied.